FROM
SHRINK TO
THINK

A MENTAL JOURNEY THROUGH
THE MEMORY JOURNEY

DANIEL GUILFOYLE

BALBOA.PRESS
A DIVISION OF HAY HOUSE

Balboa Press books may be ordered through booksellers or by contacting:

Balboa Press
A Division of Hay House
1663 Liberty Drive
Bloomington, IN 47403
www.balboapress.com
1 (877) 407-4847

Print information available on the last page.

ISBN: 978-1-9822-4257-2 (sc)
ISBN: 978-1-9822-4258-9 (e)

Balboa Press rev. date: 06/05/2020

Contents

DEDICATION

To my loving wife Erin, who has truly given me all the love and support that a man could possibly ask for in life. To my brother Matthew, who is the original inspiration for my journey into the study of memory. To my mother Lynn, the woman that has taught me the important lessons about the value of education, hard work, and knowledge. And especially to the greatest memory expert I have ever heard of, Mr. Dominic O'Brien, whose techniques and mnemonic systems have not only changed my memory abilities, but have also changed my entire life forever.

ABOUT ME

Well, hello there, nice to meet me. Let me start by introducing myself. My name is Daniel Guilfoyle, LCSW. For those of you who are not familiar with such letters and abbreviations, LCSW stands for **Licensed Clinical Social Worker**. In layman's terms, I am a *mental health therapist*. I graduated from college in 2002 with a Bachelors' Degree in Sociology, and then I completed graduate school in 2006, obtaining a Master's Degree in Social Work. I have already passed two national licensure examinations in order to fulfill the requirements needed for my clinical license in social work. I have been practicing professionally for 14 years and have had a lot of experiences in my life. And today, you are about to get your first dose of "memory therapy" from, as you guessed it, yours truly.

First, let me start off by explaining that **I am not a licensed memory coach or a certified cognitive training specialist.** I am also **not a national ranked memory champion**, though I have competed in several memory competitions before. However, despite my lack of qualifications, I, like you, was once completely unaware of the field of memory. I too was someone who was just starting out new in this particular area of study. And now, throughout the course of these upcoming pages and chapters, I will be conducting my own individual "memory" therapy sessions with you. As you read this book, you will soon find several interesting patterns that I have specifically included for you so as to provide you the complete therapeutic sense.

First, instead of giving you lots of technical and clinical terminology and definitions to read through, I will speak to you the reader <u>directly and in conversational mode</u>. As a counselor, I only want you to feel comfortable enough so that you are able to understand and comprehend what I am saying as if I were almost sitting right across from you. Second, I have included many bits of side humor throughout the chapters, to help lessen the stress and anxiety accompanied through certain situations and lessons. Most of this particular dialogue is written in parenthesis throughout random sentences. Like any good therapist, I believe it is important to find a little humor in any given situation.

Third, I have also included many important phrases, terms, words, items or important concepts throughout most of the text. Such information will either be <u>underlined</u> or listed in **bold print**. Finally, I have incorporated many specific tests and assignments for you to work on at your own pace and convenience after each lesson. I feel that as a clinician, it is very important to give my clients some type of homework to do throughout their treatment, as I will not be actually doing the work <u>for you</u>, but rather I will be going through it **with you**.

And finally, towards the end, I will be providing you the reader with some words of guidance, motivation and encouragement, as well as certain things to help you to eventually terminate from using the lessons used throughout book. In any good mental health setting, it is vitally important to let one's clients discover what they can and cannot do, as well as to focus on the client's pending strengths and potential weaknesses. It is also necessary to make sure that the client themselves feels safe and comfortable enough to disengage from treatment, and then finally go off into the real world with a new and improved fulfillness of heart and mind.

With that being said, I would like to welcome to my version of **From Shrink to Think**, where you the client will get to go on an amazing "journey" of your mind and of your memory. And I, the caring and light hearted therapist, will be "sitting" right there next to you throughout the entire process; counseling, motivating, and coaching you throughout each individual lesson. You are about to embark on an experience that will forever change the way you think about your brain and your memory. From this point on, nothing in your life will ever truly be the same again. So please come on in, sit down and relax, take a deep breath, and get ready to open your mind and your brain to new and endless possibilities.

INTRODUCTION

So, now that you are feeling rested and comfortable in your first ever "memory therapy" session, I think that it is important for us to find out exactly what your current memory looks like, and how can I help you to improve upon it. In order to determine if you think that this book is worth your time (or your money for that matter) why don't we first start off by conducting our first real "assessment" of your current level of memory competency. This is not a standardized test, nor will it ever be. This is simply an exercise to be used to help determine if your own method of memorization is already good enough to allow you to memorize multiple pieces of information quickly and accurately. Below, you will see three lists of information organized into three columns.

The first column is a series of 30 random numbers. The second column is a list of 30 English vocabulary words. And the third column is a list of 30 standard playing cards symbols. In order to prepare for this memory test, you will need to take out at least two blank sheets of paper, a pencil to write with (trust me you might need an eraser), and a stopwatch or timer. You will need to use the back of the sheets of paper possibly. On one piece of paper, you will draw column lines going straight down, number the page going down on each line from 1-30, and then copy all of the information listed in the exercise exactly as it is printed. You will use the other piece of paper as your answer sheet. You will only use the answer sheet when it is time to memorize the information. It can also be used to cover up the other columns one at a time, as you will only be doing only one memory test after another.

You will then have to memorize the first list of numbers by covering up the remaining two columns of written information with the answer sheet for this exercise. You will have only 5 minutes to memorize all of the information. Then you will turn the test paper over, and use your blank sheet of paper (the answer sheet) to record all of the information you that can remember with <u>a recall time of exactly 5 minutes</u>. Use a stopwatch for this exercise as needed. Then, once your recall time is over for the first memory test, you will turn your answer sheet over so that you cannot see the answers through the paper (make sure it is done in pencil so that you cannot see the answers through the page).

Do not worry about how well you did on the first test; you will get the chance to go over your results soon. Simply take a break for a few minutes, and then go back and repeat the same process of covering up information for the other two columns. Continue to give yourself **5 minutes to memorize each list of information with a recall time of exactly five minutes for answers**. Don't change your answers between each test. Once you have written down something on the answer sheet, leave it as it is. Make sure to record your memorization times for each list, and use a pencil to write your answers.

Once you are done, <u>record your scores</u> and see how well you did. Count out how many answers you got right for each column, and how long it took for you to do it. Remember, you have to remember the information <u>in **the exact order** that it is presented</u>, not re-organized or changed in any such way. If you are able to remember all of the information, or at least most of it in the allotted time, you probably don't need to read this book any further. Be honest with yourself, <u>no cheating, no changing answers, and no fudging scores</u>. Just give me an honest run of your actual brain power. If you score <u>anything less than 50%</u> in any of the columns, please feel free to read on and learn probably the greatest memory lesson that anyone could possible learn.

Here is the information to be memorized: Good luck and have fun. (**BY THE WAY, <u>DON'T THROW AWAY YOUR ANSWER SHEETS WHEN FINISHED.</u> HOLD ONTO THEM FOR LATER AS <u>YOU WILL BE TESTED AGAIN</u> ON THIS MATERIAL TOWARDS THE END OF THE BOOK. DON'T FEEL DEPRESSED OR UPSET WITH YOUR INITIAL SCORES. I DON'T EXPECT THAT YOU WILL BE PERFECT AT THIS THE FIRST TIME. THE POINT IS JUST TO SEE <u>HOW GOOD YOUR MEMORY CURRENTLY IS, AND TO EVENTUALLY FIGURE OUT HOW MUCH BETTER YOU CAN IMPROVE YOUR MEMORY</u> OVER THE COURSE OF THE NEXT SEVERAL CHAPTERS)**

COLUMN 1	COLUMN 2	COLUMN 3
2	Pillows	Ace Spade
4	calendar	2 of Hearts
7	office	10 of Clubs
3	flag	4 of Diamonds
6	building	6 of Clubs
5	barbecue	Jack of Diamonds
1	tombstones	Queen of Spades
9	Christmas tree	Ace of Hearts
1	soldier	2 of Clubs
1	school	9 of Hearts
7	car	8 of Clubs
4	dog	10 of Spades
2	computer	6 of Diamonds
0	library	7 of Clubs
1	baseball bat	8 of Diamonds
9	stove	Jack of Hearts
1	airplane	King of Diamonds
2	lightning	King of Clubs
2	fireworks	Queen of Hearts
5	camel	Jack of Spades
0	beer	4 of Clubs
5	TV set	2 of Spades
3	ghosts	9 of Spades
1	basketball	9 of Diamonds
1	hole	5 of Spades
7	golf clubs	5 of Clubs
7	robot	Queen of Clubs
6	chicken	8 of Spades
0	bathtub	2 of Diamonds
4	giraffe	7 of Diamonds
TOTAL TIME=	TOTAL SCORE=	TOTAL SCORE=
TOTAL TIME=	TOTAL TIME=	TOTAL TIME=

CHAPTER 1

My first real memories

Now that I have already probably stimulated your minds, or possibly managed to depress you during the first chapter of this book, let me first start out by introducing myself to you, and telling you a little bit about <u>my story of memory</u>. Again, my name is Daniel Guilfoyle, and I was born in the state of New York. When I was a little boy, I remember sitting down in front of our old television set in our house in the quiet suburb of Goshen, NY. It was not easy to watch TV back in those days (by this I mean the 1980's, not to make me feel too old in saying so), as the viewer would have to get up and manually change the channel by turning a station knob with their bare hands. Anyway, one day while my mother was preparing me and my brother to go to our usual Sunday church service, a movie suddenly came on the TV that I had tuned into. It was a movie that I had heard about in theaters before, but had never had the chance to go see. It was the blockbuster major motion picture, called "_Rain Man_".

Now, for those of you who were not fortunate enough to have ever seen such a classic picture as this, this movie tells the somewhat true yet fictionalized story of a young yet spoiled car salesman named Charlie Babbett, who discovers that he has a long lost much older brother named Raymond, who has been living in a mental institution for most of his life. When Charlie finally has the chance to meet this so-called older prodigal brother, he has no idea that the person that he is about to spend a week with, just happens to be someone who is an intellectual genius, despite his own social handicaps. Little does

Charlie know, he is about to have an experience that most people in this world could only begin to imagine.

In the movie, it turns out that Raymond has been living in a mental institution for over twenty years due to a terrible family tragedy that had occurred while Charlie was still a baby. Throughout their one-week excursion together across the county, Charlie comes to find that, although his brother Raymond is struggling with Autism and cannot seem to tie his shoes or even do his own laundry, he apparently seems to possess an extraordinary ability to use his memory in ways most people would never dream was humanly possible. In one scene, Raymond is able to calculate advanced multiplication problems, where he is easily able to figure the exact number within a few seconds. In another scene, he is shown to be able to remember the entire history of a major airline's plane crash history, simply by looking at the type of aircraft that is sitting on the runway. In both instances, Charlie is completely baffled by his brother's incredible abilities.

Throughout their adventure, Charlie realizes that, although his brother can be somewhat emotionally difficult and not so easy to live with (the scene with the lost underwear is a scene worth mentioning), he also comes to discover that his brother is a person that the rest of this world does not yet fully understand, due to his unusual cognitive abilities. Even though these two distinct brothers tend to get on each other's nerves at times, by the end of the week, poor little Charlie is finally humbled by his experiences throughout their journey, and finally begins to appreciate the complexity that is his older brother, the Rain Man. It is only after Charlie brings his brother back to the train station and returns him to the rightful place of residence, does Charlie finally being to understand the true, and yet misunderstood meaning, of the word, "**savant**".

According to most dictionaries and encyclopedias across the country, the term "savant" has variously different meanings. For our part, I am not going to overwhelm you with lots of literary terminology, but I will conclude by telling you that the definition of the word **savant** literally means "a person with significant mental disabilities that is able to demonstrate certain abilities that are far in excess of average or ordinary". During the course of this movie, Raymond, or "Rain Man" as his brother Charlie so innocently mispronounced during his childhood, demonstrates that he is capable of counting out 300 toothpicks in a matter of seconds, is able to recall the phone numbers of any person's name from a phone book after studying it for one night, and is also capable of memorizing a deck of cards in under 30 seconds. At first, when I saw this movie, I assumed it to be the work of fiction or just Hollywood directors taking the viewer's belief system to the next level. It was not until years later, that I was about to find out that such astronomical feats of mental acuity were not only real and possible, but had also been performed and demonstrated by random isolated individuals throughout the world.

Years later, when I was a teenager growing up and learning about random high school subjects in my district, I found myself struggling just to make average grades in my small-town educational curriculum. It was during that time that I started to notice that my brother, or my identical twin brother to be more specific, was starting to demonstrate intellectual abilities of his own, that I had only previously seen before during that one special movie from TV years ago. Although he claimed never to have any innate cognitive gifts or any out of this world capabilities of his own, he later showed me that not only was he was able to pass all of the advanced placement courses at our school with a near perfect GPA, but he was also able to remember random important autobiographical dates from our family's history, without having to even consult either a notebook or a piece of paper.

Each time my brother would ask me if I could remember what if anything important had happened on a specific day of the week, I would desperately ask him to get to the point and tell me what he was referring to. He would then tell me about an important or sad event that had occurred to someone in our family or in the community, and where he was standing when the event occurred. At first, I thought that he was just making up such information to make it seem as though he was gifted. But it wasn't until after I had done some fact finding by talking to others about the event, did I actually realize that he was in fact correct all along! Somehow, my brother was able to remember a specific date or event that had occurred years ago, and would simply wake up on the morning of the anniversary date for such event, and be able to recall all of the most important parts for such occasion. And he did all of this without even having to write anything. It was like his brain was a virtual journal or diary for all of our major individual life events going back years and years.

During that time of my rebellious teenage high school years, I would occasionally yet innocently joke to my friends and neighbors about my brother, usually introducing him as "my brother the Rain Man". For those people who were part of my small social circle, and had already seen the movie themselves, they vaguely understood what I was referring to when I would say such things like this. For other people that had never heard of the term "genius" or "savant" before, these people would ask my brother to do certain mental calculations or perform random memory demonstrations for them, just to see if he could do it. My brother would always excel at all of these challenges, with little to no effort.

Some people were blown away by his unusual ability for mental gymnastics; others were keener to use some hurtful and derogatory terms to describe him (these people were in fact our mutual bullies). However, as difficult as it was to be in the shadow of such a unique and intellectually talented sibling, I could not help but envy and fear the kind of life that my brother was capable of living. Though we seemed to have variously different academic interests during our childhood years, my brother seemed to have a personal gift that I would one day hope to achieve through my own individual and personal pursuits.

Also, during our teenage years, I had my first real experience in doing a memory challenge. Such challenge occurred alongside some of my best friends during some of our scout outdoor campouts. During our teenage years, my brother and I were very active in the Boy Scouts of America. We spent several years of our lives, going on different camping trips, earning lots of merit badges, learning valuable survival skills, and eventually achieving the rank of Eagle Scout. During our early times in Scouting, one of our scout masters gave us a unique memory challenge which is still used today during Boy Scout Jamborees. It is a game commonly referred to in the scouting program as **Kim's Game**.

Kim's Game is a game where you are taught how to use your memory skills and observational skills under timed pressured exercise.

In order to do this, our scoutmaster would collect a number of survival related camping items, and then place these items under a tarp or large sheet. He would then have the scouts gather around and uncover the tarp for only 1 minute. Then he would again cover the items back up, and then have each scout write down as many items they could remember on a sheet of paper. The scout with the most correct items would have then demonstrated the best observational and recollection skills, and that person was later given a prize for such accomplishment. Also, this game helped us to become better "prepared" for our future campouts, as we would normally lay out all of our personal belongings on the ground, count them up and memorize them, and then finally proceed to pack them all in our backpacks. I did not realize it at that time, but I was getting my first "real world" test in memory related skills.

Now, lets' fast forward about twenty years ahead into the future, right up to the year 2016. Here I was, in my late-thirties, happily married and working to pay the bills at home. It seemed as though all the experiences of my high school and Boy Scout days were but just a distant memory for me. Yet, there would be times when my brother would still call me at home, where my wife and I would be enjoying the comfort of a wonderful evening meal or just a relaxing hour of television. He would again ask me if could remember what had happened to both of us possibly ten, fifteen or even twenty years ago. And again, I would simply ask him what exactly he was referring to. And like always, he would tell me about another event in either of our lives that had happened on that day with complete accuracy.

Now of days, we are lucky enough to have more technological inventions in our lives, such as the internet and I Phones. So I naturally assumed that he was just looking up such information by some other means, and then just relaying it back to me. However, when he was able to remember a specific family vacation or birthday party where there were no actual pictures taken, I realized that he could not be using any type of electronic technology to help recall such information. Again, he had been using his long-term memory in order to access such information from years ago. Like always, he never seemed to stop amazing me with his amazing memory talent. However, I too was about to embark upon a miraculous and unexpected memory "**journey**" of my own, headed towards the same peaks of memory that he was capable of climbing. (don't worry, I will explain the significance of this word in a later chapter).

In 2016, I was going through some very difficult challenges in my life. At that time, I had already graduated ten years earlier with a _master's degree in social worker_ (**MSW**), and was actively working full-time at a state correctional facility. In addition, I was also dealing with some chronic medical issues of my own, as well as struggling with unresolved bouts of anxiety and depression that I still continue to cope with to this day. Each day that I had to report to work, I was constantly exposed to various terrifying experiences. Violent mentally ill inmates, powerful and intimidating prison guards, constantly hostile and belligerent co-workers, as well as unhealthy and filthy working conditions, filled my work with unending moments of constant dread.

Day in and day out, the endless hours of constant fear, anxiety, pain, anger, and suffering, continued to plague my mind and body more and more. As time went on, working in such an oppressive and dangerous environment began to prove almost too much for me to handle. There were many days when I would not be able to eat or sleep well, my stomach was constantly hurting all the time, and I was socially isolating from my friends and family. Most nights before I went to sleep, disturbing dark thoughts would enter my mind just before I closed my eyes. (Yes, _dark thoughts,_ I cannot explain to you the reader what this means) I soon began to fear that that there was no real "escape" from this _prison_ of memory that was constantly torturing me. It seemed as though I really needed some help before it was too late.

Being the ever-diligent therapist that I was, I decided to go into treatment myself in order to help deal with some of my own personal issues before things got any worse. During my therapy sessions, my psychologist would ask me whether I had any other recreational hobbies or interests that I could pursue that would help me in my treatment sessions. At first, I was not sure where to start looking, as there were many choices out there. From using therapeutic coloring books, to journaling, running outside, or even meditating, I tried everything yet nothing really seemed to make a difference in my battle to maintain sanity. I realized that while these activities would occasionally take my mind off of my pain, they could not help me to truly "forget" my inner torment. I needed to feel good about myself again, and something had to change soon before I started to sink down into that dark and dismal hole of depression. Finally, one day in 2016, another great movie on television caught my eye. And that one particular film would forever change my life, and start me off on the path to a new and exciting adventure of my mind.

In the hit 2011 Hollywood blockbuster film called "*Limitless*", the main character is a struggling and unemployed book writer in NYC named Eddie Morra. In the movie, Eddie is a young man who is crippled with writer's block, as he has not produced a significant book or piece of literary work for several years. During an unexpected yet fortuitous encounter with his ex-brother in law Vernon, Eddie is given a sample of a not so FDA approved nootropic pill referred to as "NZT 48". Although this pill really looks no different from a typical aspirin or breath-mint, he decides to ingest it anyway and to see how it affects him. And in just a few minutes, he is able to defuse a conflict between himself and his landlord's angry wife by remembering the exact subject matter of a book that he had glanced at several years ago. He later goes on to completely clean out his apartment, as well finding the ability to write out half of his unpublished manuscript, before the pill finally wears off.

The next day, not seeming to have any of his previous profound cognitive powers, Eddie delivers his manuscript to his publisher in the hopes that he can keep his job. Much to his surprise, when he returns home a few hours later, he has received several messages from his publisher, lauding and praising his book as his best work yet. From that point on, Eddie is determined to continue to take this supposed "miracle" pill each day in order to take on the corporate world and thereby establish himself as being "limitless".

Although I am not advocating that in order to get a phenomenal memory one must seek out the holy grail of cognitive nootropics. I was just however intrigued at the possibility of one day having a memory that was either similar or even better that the one Bradley Cooper demonstrated in the movie. So, now I had an idea about what new hobby I could possibly embark upon that could be used as the key to not only the resolution of my mental health conflict, but also the chance for me to make something extraordinary of myself. I realized that I was already in my late thirties and was not prepared to spend years and years simply trying to make a few moderate improvements in my brain. I needed a quick answer to the age old question that I had asked myself years earlier when I was a child. And that question was about how to truly achieve memory mastery. It was then that I decided to look up some information about memory improvement techniques, and to try to learn from some of the world's greatest mnemonists, about how to unlock the unused potential within my brain.

After I had spent some time scavenging helplessly around the Internet, hoping to find some answer to my questions about savant syndrome and photographic memory, I was finally able to locate a website that dealt with memory competitions from around the world. On one particular site, the main article dealt with an annual memory sport competition known as the "World Memory Championship". In this entry, I was able to find out information about the various people who were some of the world's greatest mnemonists and memory athletes from years past. I desperately wanted to find someone from that list whom I was sure had the answers to the questions I had about memory improvement. As I gazed through the short list of past winners and competitors, one particular name really seemed to catch my eye.

The name that always seemed to come up each time I glanced at the list of past winners, was one particular English gentleman named **Dominic O'Brien**. Once I clicked on his name and read through his biography, I knew that this was the person who had the answers to all the questions about memory that I had been looking for. Not only was this English gentleman the winner of the very first World Memory Championship back in 1991, he had also won it a total of 8 times over the course of thirteen years, either placing in first or sometimes second or third! It seemed as though this man must have the greatest memory ever recorded in world history, as he had been capable of winning such a prestigious and highly competitive tournament so many times in a row. I had finally uncovered my own personal "holy grail" of memory, and I knew what books I wanted to read in order to improve my own memory.

Before I continue, I would like to take a moment and express my warm and sincere thanks and appreciation to this great and powerful man in the world of memory sports. **Mr. Dominic O' Brien's** books and articles have literally changed my life and opened up new windows of possibility for me. I would not be writing this book today without the guidance and suggestions of this marvelous memory icon. In addition, I want to make sure that you reader understand **that I am not taking credit for his particular memory system** as it is entirely his creation. I am only simply telling you the reader about how I have utilized his memory techniques for my own individual purposes. I do not have ownership of his methods; I am simply a student of it. So, that being said let me tell you what happened when I finally got around to ordering two of his books online.

Once I had purchased the books, I immediately started out by reading both of them. At first, I was a little bit confused and nervous about the subject matter. I almost expected such books to only tell me that the secret to a great memory was possibly just hard work, maybe a little patience, lots of sleep and a lot less stress. However, I was in for quite a surprise once I finished reading the first three chapters of one of these books. For it was in those first few chapters, did the author finally let me know that I was capable of doing something quite amazing with my memory.

In those first three chapters, he challenged his readers to memorize a list of twenty numbers and thirty vocabulary words, each list in only five minutes a piece, and then to recall such information on a piece of paper later. I got out my stop watch, put on my ear phones, and got started. After my five minutes was up with each list, I took out my notebook and a pen, and used whatever creative memory I had to at that point, to conjure up all the information that was listed in my brain. Needless to say, when I was finished writing my answers, I was deeply disappointed with the results. I could not remember even half of the information listed, and I had used up all the time that was allowed for this exercise. At first, I felt like throwing the book in the garbage and crying myself to sleep. However, after this first exercise was over, Mr. O'Brien instructed his readers to continue to read the next three chapters of the book, and then to try the exercise again. It was inside those upcoming three chapters, did he finally introduce me to a particular memory technique referred to as the "journey method", "the method of loci" or the "memory method". It was this method that would prove to be a life changer for me. (I will go over how this system works in a later chapter).

After reading through those next three chapters, and finally understanding what Dominic was referring to in regards to the "journey method", I then set about the task of trying the initial memory exercise once again. As it had been a few days since I last had tried it, all of the information that I had memorized before was completely erased from my mind (we will talk about this particular phenomenon later on). So I felt much safer in repeating my past performance. Only this time, I was armed and ready with a whole new approach to the task at hand. So, I got out my stop watch and my ear plugs, and made my second attempt at improving my memory by looking through the lists of information again. After the timer had finally gone off, I was shocked to realize that I had only needed a little more than half the time allotted for this exercise. I calmly grabbed my paper and pen, and proceeded to write out all the answers that I could remember.

After checking over my work, I was completely blown away by what I had done! Not only had I done better on the second attempt, but I had actually gotten a near "perfect" score with still some time left to spare. I had not only improved my memory over the course of reading just a few chapters, I had literally doubled or even possibly tripled my mental recall abilities. I had increased my previous score by a factor of two, and was using only half as much time as was needed. This was the moment that I referred to my own personal memory journey, as my "light bulb" or "ah ha" moment. This would be the moment when I knew that I had discovered a new part of my brain that had lain dormant for so many years, and now had only just been unlocked for the very first time.

From there, I decided that I would like to take my memory skills to even greater heights, rather than just simply practicing such exercises in the safety of my own home. It was then that I decided that I wanted to enter the **USA Memory Championship** in 2018. As I had only started using this technique just a year earlier, I was not sure how well I was going to do out there, or what I was about to get myself into. I traveled several hours away to a wonderful hotel in Pennsylvania, where my wife and I stayed overnight. It was in the lobby of such hotel the following morning that I was able to locate the actual room where I would be able to participate in probably the greatest memory tournament in the United States. The day proved to be quite an amazing experience for me. After a few hours of intense memory competitions and challenges, such as recalling cards, words, names and faces, as well as poetry, I was able to come out in 11th place overall, out of almost 50 competitors, some of whom were previous winners. Although I did not win such tournament, I did better than I thought I could ever have done.

Before I get too far ahead, let me tell you a little history about the **USA Memory Championship.** Each year during the spring season, there is usually a large competition hosted in either New York City or Pennsylvania, where at least 80 to 100 people from across the county can come together in one room and compete against each other in the most coveted memory competition in the nation. It is called the USA Memory Championship, and it has been hosted for over 23 years by a great team of moderators and presenters. In this tournament, there are multiple different rounds of competition that pit memory athletes against each other, to see who has the mental capacity to remember the most amount of information both the fastest and most accurately.

There are at least four different rounds that a person would have to pass in order to get into the semi-final rounds. In the beginning of the competition, players have to remember different pictures of people's names and faces in 15 minutes. After the initial time is up, the person would be given a whole new packet of pictures of the same faces, only in a different order and without the associated names attached to them. Then the person would be given 20 minutes to write down the names of every face that they could remember, but in a different order than on the memorization sheet. Then, the next round would be speed numbers, where the person would have to memorize as many digits as possible within five minutes. Here, 20 digits are placed in each row with 25 rows per page. After memorization, memory athletes are given 10 minutes for recall. For every complete row memorized in order, 20 points are given. For every row that has any mistakes 0 points are given.

Later on would be <u>speed cards</u>, where the contestants would have to memorize the order of an entire shuffled deck of playing cards as quickly as possible. A judge sits by the memory athlete with a stopwatch to record the time. After memorization, the person is given 5 minutes for recall. After the recall, the memory athletes are given a second set of cards in perfect order, and are then told to place those cards in the same order as the first deck memorized. Two trials are given and the best score is counted. The person with the fastest time wins the most points.

Finally, the last part of the initial competition is <u>poetry</u>, where each person has to memorize an unpublished poem within 15 minutes. 20 minutes are given for recall, in which the competitors must transcribe the poem, word for word, from beginning to end, in the same format as the original. Each person is allowed to omit 2 consecutive lines from the poem. Scoring is graded based on correct spelling, punctuation, and capitalization. Each line has its own number of points and each mistake made will result in zero points for the line where the mistake was found.

And yet this only gets you to the semi-final rounds. After this strenuous test of memory is completed, there are still <u>three more rounds of competition</u> left to be had. After the first four events, eight mental athletes are left to advance to the final round of Championship events. A round-robin tournament style is used for elimination. Three Competitors are eliminated after the first event, two after the second, and two during the third to determine the final Memory Champion. During this afternoon sequence, the first category for memory would be <u>spoken words</u>, where each person has to memorize a list of 200 words in order in 15 minutes. After the period of memorization is over, memory athletes are called by random, and are given 15 seconds to orally recite the first word of the first column, proceeding through all of the columns. The words continue consecutively down the list and the first person to either recall the wrong word or not remember the actual word at least three times is eliminated.

After this round is over, then the next stage of competition, called

"Three Strikes You're Out" begins. In here, the five remaining memory athletes left in this round are given 15 minutes to hear and review personal facts about 6 strangers. Such facts for each stranger might include things such as their addresses, phone numbers, pets, favorite hobbies, favorite cars, and favorite foods. This round is scored like spoken words, but each person is given three strikes before elimination. Finally, the last round of competition is called "Double Decker", where the final three memory athletes are asked to memorize not one, but **TWO** decks of cards, back to back, from beginning to end, in less than five minutes. Then each of the final three contestants is verbally asked to recall each card in the decks out loud in a round robin style of recall. The first person to get one answer wrong is eliminated, until there is only one contestant left standing as the new winner of the USA Memory Championship.

Though I did not win the championship that year, and was not allowed to compete in the actual finals, just being able to demonstrate my memory abilities to not only my wife and to the other competitions, but also to this country as a whole, made me feel like I had just achieved something that I had only read about before. I was now officially a "memory athlete" as I had competed in a real live tournament and had passed each and every memory challenge without quitting or failing. I then went to compete again in 2019 and finished in 15th out of over 55 competitors, alongside some other previous winners and a few new athletes who broke several national and world records. I will be coming back to compete again at the 2020 competition, where I hope to do even better than I did before and possibly make it to the finals, where I will finally be able to sit next to the 8 greatest memory athletes of this country.

Well, enough about me and memory competitions. You did not come here to listen to me talk about myself, my past, or my previous "journeys". We are here to talk about you, and how you would like to improve or enhance your memory abilities. However, throughout the course of this book, I will include little bits and pieces of autobiographical information about myself and other important people in my life, as each story ultimately relates to a different topic of memory in my life. And you will see how each and every major event in my life, from my

CHAPTER 2

What is memory, and what are the different types and styles

Before you start to think that I am trying to sell you the idea of possibly achieving a photographic or eidetic memory, let me just try to clarify a few things for you about what the concept truly is. First of all, terms such as *eidetic memory* and *photographic memory* are commonly used almost interchangeably, but they are also distinguished from each other. For instance, with regards to the term **eidetic memory**, this idea would best describe a person who can have an almost *perceptual mental image* snapshot or a "photograph" of an event or a piece of information locked away in their long term memory. However, eidetic memory is not limited to just visual aspects of memory as it can also include auditory memories as well as various sensory aspects such as smell and taste. In layman's terms, **eidetic memory** is having the ability to remember an image in one's mind with such great detail, clarity, and accuracy, that it feels as though the image were still being perceived by the person through their own physical eyes.

The type of people who have reported to have eidetic memories continues to both intrigue and fascinates the average skeptics out there who wonder how such a person came to be how they are. For those rare and lucky few naturals in the world (the majority of memory athletes have to train and condition themselves to have such an ability) who possess the "gift" as we call it, they report that after they have remembered something either seen or heard, that a vivid after-image still continues to linger in their visual field within their eyes. This vivid after-image appears to scan across their visual field as it is being described. Contrary to ordinary mental imagery, eidetic images are usually externally projected, or experienced as outward rather than just in the mind. Some even claim that the clearness and dimensions of this so called image begins to fade within several minutes after the removal of the actual visual object from their senses. For some, they state that they can see the image in their minds just as accurately as the average person could describe the details of a painting immediately in front of us.

In contrast, the term **photographic memory** itself can be described as a person having the ability to recall pages of informational text, numbers, words or letters, in great detail, _without the actual visualization image_ that comes with eidetic memory. It can be described as having the ability to briefly look at a page of information, and then recite it later perfectly from memory. This type of ability has never been proven to exist, and is considered a popular myth in most parts of the world. In order to accurately constitute photographic memory, the visual recall itself would have to persist in the person's mind without the use of any mnemonics skills or other cognitive strategies.

This explains why some people falsely tend to think of national and world champion memory athletes as having photographic memory. Various cases of such memory have been reported that rely on the person having such technical skills or methods, and are erroneously attributed to photographic memory. Certain TV characters come to mind when I think about people with photographic memory, such as Sheldon Cooper from Big Bang Theory and Mike Ross from Suits.

One example of extraordinary memory abilities that could possibly be attributed to eidetic memory comes from the example of the ability of world chess grandmasters due to their required need to memorize complex positions of chess pieces on a chess board. I myself have never learned how to play anything more than average checkers, and even then I lost a few matches in my youth. However, when it comes to these special chess prodigies, it has been discovered that these individuals could somehow recall surprising amounts of information about each game they played, usually far more information than could be remembered by non-experts. This would thereby suggest that they might have eidetic skills. However, when these chess experts have been presented with arrangements of chess pieces that could never actually occur in a game, their recall of the information was no better than the non-experts.

This means that the chess masters had somehow developed an ability to effectively organize certain types of information in large sequences, rather than simply possessing innate eidetic abilities. I guess it goes to show you that, when you think inside the box,(or in this case inside the chess board) there is only a limited or finite amount of information that you can play with. For those of you interested in seeing any movies or films about such fortunate chess prodigies, I would highly recommend either "Searching for Bobby Fisher" or "Life of a King". (Trust me; you will see what I am talking about when you watch them)

However, there are other individuals in this world who have even more rare cases of exceptional memory abilities. There are individuals who have been identified and diagnosed as having a condition known as "**hyperthymesia**". These people are able to remember very intricate details of their own personal lives in perfect detail. However, this ability does not seem to extend to other, non-autobiographical information, such as world history or dates. It seems as though the person with this condition can have vivid recollections about the names of people that they were in contact with, what they were wearing, or how they were feeling on a specific date in history many years in the past.

Some researchers have even ruminated over the fact that patients with this type of rare condition often seems similar to people with obsessive-compulsive disorder. People of this type may additionally have depression which stems from their inability to forget unpleasant memories and experiences from the past. However, it is a mistake to assume that hyperthymesia itself actually has anything to do with eidetic memory abilities. This is due to the fact that the person with this condition is actually unable to control or determine when the information will be processed by their minds; it is as if they could be classified as having more of a **video-recorded memory** rather than a photographic memory. One great example of a TV series that deals with an individual who struggles with this type of disorder, is a

TV series called Unforgettable, where the lead actress plays a police detective with the unusual ability to remember all the details of any crime that happened from years ago, without being able to stop the memories from coming.

Now that we have dispelled with some of the myths and beliefs, as well as some of the facts, regarding such unique and rare memory traits, let's start by getting back to the basic question that most people will need to know in order to better understand what memory is. And that question is, **how does memory actually work and why**? One point that is crucial in the field of cognitive neuroscience is how information and mental experiences are actually physically coded and represented within the brain. Scientists have gained much knowledge about the neurons of the brain from studies of brain plasticity, but most of the research has only focused on simple ability learning in normal everyday skills, such as math and reading.

There is much less information about the neural changes that are involved in more complex examples of memory, such as declarative memory, which requires the storage of facts and events through auditory memory. There are several kinds of memory that we all use at any given time, all of which depends on certain things such as variously different types of concrete information, differing underlying mechanisms, unknown process functions, and distinct modes of acquisition. It can be expected that different areas of the brain are able to support and promote different types of memory systems. I guess it goes to show you that the most highly complex and complicated computer system in the whole world itself actually *exists right inside of our heads*, and we still don't completely know how it truly works.

Now that I have possibly overloaded your minds with various bits of information about the brain and memory, let me just try to clarify a few things to you to make it simpler for you to understand what this is all about. In this book, there are only two types of memory that I will be working with you on as well as showing you how to improve upon. The two types of memory that this book deals with are called short-term and long-term memory. **Short-term memory** is also known as **working memory**. Short-term memory allows for a person to recall information for a short period of time such as several seconds to a minute without rehearsal. This capacity is also very limited. However, many of us don't realize exactly how much information we can store inside of our short term memory before it starts to get cloudy. For any person who has ever wondered why our phone numbers are only seven digits, there is a mnemonic reason for such limitations.

Several famous scientists conducted experiments back in the 1950's, showing that the storage amount for short-term memory for most people was only about seven items, possibly even as low as five. (By the way, the famous paper written about this theory was called, "**The magical number 7±2**"). This is why most phone numbers for people in the US are only 7 digits long, and not 8 or 9 digits. And the only real *magic* that can ever come from the number 7 itself would probably come from somewhere inside a casino. (I like to hit the slots whenever I get a chance)

Just think about the fact that we only have the ability to easily recall several bits of information in our memory before the rest of the information simply goes out of our heads. However, before you start comparing your brain to that of caveman or start looking for that extra cup of coffee, let me help you realize that you already know how to organize information in your heads much more efficiently than you think. It has been told that memory capacity can be easily be increased through a process called **chunking**. (I tend to think of a chocolate bar when I hear this) I know that this might seem funny at first when you hear it, but take my word for it; this process is a lot more effective than you think it is. For example, in recalling a ten-digit telephone number, a person could easily chunk the numbers into three different groups: first, the area code (such as 123), then a three-digit chunk of numbers (456) and lastly a four-digit chunk of numbers(7890).

The method of remembering telephone numbers is far more effective than attempting to remember a string of 10 digits. The reason for this is because we are able to chunk the information into meaningful groups of numbers, with each group of numbers having its own special meaning, purpose, and importance. Most phone numbers have to start off with the area codes, and then followed shortly by the rest of the numbers in the previously mentioned order. When you really think about it, is your name really a name, or is it simply just a random string of letters that are considerately chunked together to make a sound out of? My name is spelled Daniel; however it is also spelled (**D A N I E L**). Ever notice how hard it was to read the second one as compared to the first one. Even the words in this book could be written as separate letters with no discernible connections.

It would probably take you days or weeks to fully understand what was actually being written. However, with the innate ability to simply make information somehow connected, linked or "chunked" together in variously sorted groups, we are now more able to recall and process any type of written information in front of us as opposed to just seeing randomly isolated rows and bits of letters and numbers.

Interesting enough, what you don't already realize is that most of the information that we normally utilize each and every day, has already been chunked for us beforehand in order to make it easier to recall for future use. Whenever I want to think of the 26 letters of the alphabet, instead of simply saying all the letters one at a time, I usually find myself singing the letters to the lovely beat of an old familiar song I learned as a child: **the alphabet song**.

In this song, the first several letters are mentioned from A-G, and then there is a pause, and then the next group of letters follows from H-P. Somehow, when we were children, this made it easier and a lot more fun for us to remember our letters as opposed to mechanically rehearsing the sequence from start to finish. And at the end of the alphabet song, there was always some limerick that ended with "now I know my ABC's, won't you come and play with me?" This always made me feel better once I was done, as I felt as though I was still a child again, learning those beginner's level lessons once again. Try to imagine what if any other basic information you have already heard about that has already been condensed for us in the form of songs or limericks. Try to think about the letters on a music scale if you would like, I remember an old song about that for the same reasons.

The next major area of memory that I will be talking about is something many of us have heard of, called **long-term memory**. Basically speaking, <u>long term memory</u> is the having the ability to recall and remember a large amount of information at any given time after a long waiting period of at least a few months or even several years, with almost perfect accuracy. My brother and I used to listen to comedy tapes of our favorite comedians of the day back in the 1980's. Strange to think that even after all of these years since we last listened to such tapes, we can still recall all of the phrases and sayings whenever we feel like entertaining a crowd. The way it works is like this; the more important something is to us, the more we are likely to recall it again when we need to.

We are species of a different sort, in that we actively chose what is, and more importantly, what is not important information to us. This selective ability allows us to create our own little memory "file folder" of valuable Intel that we often pull out in the real world when the time is needed. Think about your all-time favorite movie as a kid that you have not seen in many years and ask yourself if you could remember many of the lines from it. Chances are you probably can, while the next person sitting close to you probably does not even remember the title of the picture you quoted.

When it comes to long term memory, the main question that many of us ask ourselves is how is it that not everybody can remember the same information as long and as accurately as everyone else? Because like I said earlier, we all have different and distinct interests in our lives. The information that most easily peaks our interest is the same information that our brains are most hungry to consume and hold onto for later usage. Those countless classes we took in high school where we asked ourselves, "when are we ever going to have to use this in the future", are probably the same classes that we remember the least amount of information from as grown-ups.

However, just imagine if you could make any piece of information in this world into somewhat interesting to you, simply by trying to connect that information to something else in your life that you are both familiar with and excited about. Just imagine how much easier it would be to recall any bland or boring topic of information simply by "linking" that information to something else in your life of greater importance to you. (Hint hint, that is the main lesson that you are about to learn in the upcoming chapter, which will change the way you think about your memory forever.

CHAPTER 3

Mnemonics, method of loci, and memory palaces

In order to be sure that we can get started on the right step, let's first discuss what the term "**mnemonics**" truly means and why it is so important to the field of memory. Without getting into any clinical or advanced terminology, the true meaning of the word "<u>mnemonics</u>" basically describes what particular methods or strategies people chose to use for the purposes of learning, processing, or understanding of information, so that such information is easier for the person to memorize and remember for a later time. Certain mnemonics that we all grew up with consisted on simple things, like abbreviations or rhymes, that were used to help us to remember specific facts in very hilarious and often absurd ways.

The earlier example of the alphabet song is just one example of a mnemonic that we all grew up with. In addition, when I was taking math classes in high school, one of my teachers used a particular mnemonic in class that read "**P**lease **E**xcuse **M**y **D**ear **A**unt **S**ally". What he was trying to teach us had nothing to do with possibly trying to ignore any embarrassing mishaps or mistakes from some fictional aunt named Sally. Instead, in order to avoid confusion, he asked each of us to look at the first letter of each word and then try to remember the initials. (**<u>PEMDAS</u>**) By repeating the sentence to ourselves, we were able to isolate the first initials for each word in correct order. Then he explained that this principle was something that applied to basic mathematical principles involving addition, subtraction, division and multiplication. By making up this funny and humorous story about an accident prone aunt named Sally, the class was able to remember this mathematical principle much easier than if it were explained to us in more scientific and obviously mind-numbing terms.

When I was in 11th grade, I was studying high school level geography of both the US and other related countries. In that class, my teacher wanted to know if any of the students in my junior class, were able to recall the names of all of the Great Lakes in the United States. At first, we all sat them, closed our eyes and tried to recall such obvious information to the best of our abilities. We had earlier learned this information from the previous lesson, and were hoping that the names would all come back to us if we concentrated hard enough. Unfortunately, we were not able to remember all of the names; some of the students did not recall even a single name correctly. Finally, my teacher drew a weird picture of five large houses or "**HOMES**" all floating on a long river bed. He then stated that the names of the Great Lakes were actually Lake **H**uron, Lake **O**ntario, Lake **M**ichigan, Lake **E**rie and Lake **S**uperior. We then asked him how this type of information could be relevant to a simple picture of several houses floating on a river bed. He then stated that all we needed to do was to define the pictures as being "<u>HOMES</u>", not houses, and that we would eventually remember all of the names of such lakes correctly.

Well, he was right about that, as shortly after that lesson, all of us were able to recall the names of the lakes in different orders, without making any mistakes. And just like that, I began to understand the basic principles of <u>mnemonics</u>. All you had to do was think about something **that you already knew about, and try to attach it to something that you did not already know about**. This is the basic foundation of mnemonics, and most children who are in school, will usually use simpler patterns such as rhymes, initials, abbreviations or odd sentences, to help them recall valuable pieces of textbook information for similar purposes. (just think about what life was like before we ever had emoji icons for such purposes)

For those of you who assumed that this book would just be giving you all the intricate and voluminous details about the inner workings of your memory and mind, you can try and relax for now. The lessons on how the brain works and how memory itself functions will no longer be explored any further in this book. Instead, let's talk about the real magical secret trick behind some of the greatest memory athletes of our time. And that hidden secret that we have all been waiting to learn about, probably the most important memory method you will ever have to learn, is **the method of loci**. The **method of loci** is a method of memory enhancement which uses visualizations through the use of both spatial memory and familiar information, in regards to one's personal environment, in order to quickly and efficiently recalls information.

The method of loci is also referred to as the **memory journey**, **memory palace**, or **mind palace technique**. This method is a mnemonic device that was used back in ancient Roman and Greek times. (Remember, there was a time where things like computers, notebooks, pens, pencils or even paper did not exist). What was one to do about the formidable task of having to recall information again at a later date without having something else used to help in the retrieval process? Just because we use the term "recorded history", does not mean that history only started upon the invention of paper and pencil. In regards to this technique, the person would memorize the layout of some "palace" building, the arrangement of various buildings on a street, or any geographical location which was composed of a number of different objects located inside of it. And then the person would try to recall where each room or domestic article was positioned in relation to another one, such as doors, walls, steps and windows. In this way, the person would be mentally going over the architecture and layout of their own particular palace of memory.

The idea of a "memory palace" goes back all the way to the days of the ancient Greeks and Romans. It was from there that the origins of the memory palace technique would come to actually change history forever. One of the earliest known stories or fables about the usage of the memory method palace technique comes from the story of **Simonides of Ceos**, a famous and powerful early Greek philosopher. Although this story might sound somewhat disturbing and tragic, it describes in detail the birthplace and origins of this unique memory technique.

According to legend, after being invited to a banquet to recite a poem, the poet Simonides of Ceos chanted the lyrics out loud and did not finish the rest of the poem, for he had already memorized it. But when his host stated he would only pay him half of what was owed if he did not finish the sermon, he decided not to honor such request. It was during that time that Simonides was also hosting a large party at one of his famous yet dilapidated banquet halls. He had purposely arranged and organized what rooms and what seats each person was assigned to sit in, and asked that each person remain in their respective areas for the duration of the party. There were dozens and dozens of fellow guests at his party, some of whom he had never met before. A few moments later Simonides was given a message that two men were waiting outside the banquet hall for him to come out. So Simonides went outside to speak to these men and find out what their business with him was.

All of a sudden, without any warning, the ground itself shook and the banquet hall roof crashed on top of his guests, killing them all. Simonides was powerless to stop the eventual carnage occurring to his party guests. The victims were so badly injured that they were not identifiable due to their injuries, and most people were too afraid to go into the rubble to locate any of their missing loved one. Yet Simonides was able to aide in the identification of all of the members of his party, by means of recalling where each person sat during the banquet and where their bodies were later located. Eventually, he was able to positively identify the names and locations of all of his houseguests on that terrible day, without making a single mistake. To think about it, we owe all of our thanks and gratitude for this incredible memory technique which was based upon an unfortunate Greek tragedy. Weird isn't it?

Now before you decide to put this book away and start mourning for the losses of those innocent Greek souls, ask yourself if you have ever had the opportunity to use a mnemonic technique such as the memory palace in your own time, under less horrific circumstances obviously. In order to better understand this phenomenon more clearly, just try to imagine yourself driving a car on the same route each and every day for a long time. After a while, you start to go on what is commonly referred to as "**auto pilot**", meaning that you don't remember even getting into the car, only that you somehow ended up at your final destination. Now try to imagine that one of the streets you encounter on your route is under construction, and you have to take a detour.

Suddenly, you become much more aware and alert to all of your surroundings, perhaps getting nervous and anxious about where to turn next. At this point, you are literally paying attention to whatever you can see in order to help guide and navigate you back to your original course of travel. For many of us who grew up without the benefit of Internet maps website or GPS (yes there was a time when people actually had to navigate using road map books, I still remember those days), this seems like an easy and non-stressful situation, as most technological devises will simply guide you back to your comfort zones. So, why bother trying to pay attention to anything for that reason, when the machine can do most of the work for you instead of using your brains?

This idea of navigational travel also falls in line with one of my earlier statements about a subject known as **memory pegs**, or as you would call them, reference guides. Such methods make it easier to simply recall information as opposed to struggling hard to memorize it for future reasons. This method of memory is asking you to virtually "walk" through a large location without having to actually get up and move around it physically. If you ever have the chance to take a taxi cab in a major city anywhere in the world, remember that not all taxi drivers used to have GPS or map books in the front seat. These original "navigators" of the metropolis had to rely upon their visual-spatial memory in order to remember the best routes to take to get from one destination to another. They were the original human GPS's of their time, as they would have to recall how to change directions and tactics, while simultaneously paying attention to their driving of the car itself. I one time had to take a cab ride in NYC from the east side to the west side, and the driver encountered three different detours along the way, and yet somehow managed to get me to my destination without using a map or a GPS. (What is to say that some of us could not try to achieve the same thing as they did?)

In using the method of loci, when the person wants to remember several items in a row, the person mentally 'walks' through these different locations, or loci, in their imagination and then tries to connect each piece of information to each separate location, by forming an image connecting that item to any feature of the location. This process works because what we are really doing, <u>is to try to connect something we do know (the journey location) to something we have yet to learn (the new information)</u>. The ability to recall or retrieve this information is achieved by simply 'walking' through the journey again, and as you go from one location to the next, you then "arrive" at the desired items in our minds when you reach the next location. It is best to use locations or buildings that one is most used to or familiar with, such as a relative's house or a place of work.

These types of places tend to have more sentimental and emotional value than others, as we have become acquainted with the dimensions and architecture of such places. You will notice as you walk from one location to another, that there is always another piece of information to recall that has a different color, shape, texture or quality to it from the previous one. Perhaps the items to remember are things like lightbulbs, magnifying glasses, shopping carts and cameras. Imagine walking down a pathway, and around each turn or bend, a new item "pops" up as you continue along your journey. This mental "<u>filing cabinet</u>" system thereby can provide an efficient organizational system for the information you want to remember in the short term, and makes it an easier for the future retrieval and later review of such information.

In terms of organizational skills, any work-related information that you want to remember could be "stored" in any memory journeys that are *related* to your work site. And any personal or family related information could be stored in any family related memory journeys as well for future references. Some places might be easier to recall than others. It helps to either sit down and be alone with your thoughts for a few minutes and mentally walk through what you think the palace used to look like from your own perspective. Places that you have visited or lived more recently will be easier to recall as opposed to other places that you have not seen in many years. I for one have sat down by myself and drawn out a sketch or written down a list of the various locations within all of my memory palaces, so that I have a reference guide to use when I want to remember my "routes" throughout each journey.

I called this a journey journal. (I will explain this concept at a later time). Don't' worry, you don't have to remember every single detail of every room in your palaces. (this is not Architectural Digest) All you have to care about is the relation of each room or location to each other, such as where the hallway is in relation to the room or where the stairway is in relation to the hallway for each memory palace. It if helps, draw out a rudimentary blue print of a house the way that you remember it, so that you can easily navigate from one location to the next.

Before we get too far ahead of ourselves, in order to better be able to utilize a memory palace effectively, there is one exercise that I would like to give you before we talk any further about memory journeys. And this exercise involves using your imagination or the ability to use your "**inner senses**". As you already know, you have <u>5 active senses</u>: **sight, smell, taste, touch, and hearing**. For now, I would like for you to picture the following image in your mind and to use your inner senses to describe everything about it that you can. This will help you to strengthen your inner imagination and be better able to create images or pictures in your head much easier so that you can utilize such subliminal energies. Although we are all well grounded in reality and have a hard time conjuring up images that are not real, it is essentially this ability of cognitive imagination that is vitally important for the student of memory to be able to remember information more effectively.

For your first exercise in imagination, try to an <u>elephant holding a delicious ice cream snack</u>. First, I want you to try to imagine how the ice cream must taste when it put it in your mouth. Is it cold, creamy, sugary, or warm? Now, try to imagine what it feels like when the ice cream is melting on your skin, does it feel sticky, gooey, or wet and drippy? Then, try to think about how the ice cream smells when you take a sniff of it. Do you smell the flavors, the sprinkles, or the cone itself? How about now we take a peek at the elephant with the ice cream done. What can you tell about him? If you stood close to the elephant, how do you think his skin would feel? Would it be hard, full of scales, dry, flaky, or coarse? What would he sound like to you if he made a roar? Would it sound loud, soft, high or low? Finally, what would he smell like to you? Would he be clean and fresh, or dirty and stinky? Close your eyes, concentrate hard, and get the picture in your head. Do this exercise for at least one to two minutes and let your imagination take you to a whole new world of inner sensory. This process is called **imaging** in the field of memory sports, and it helps to better recall information as though you are watching a cartoon in your head.

Now that you have already started to grasp the subject of what a memory palace is supposed to look like, and what mental imagery feels like, don't get too excited; you are about half way through the "journey" itself (no pun intended). At this point, now you will have to learn how to encode or decipher the information that you want to remember. Since the memory journey relates to something you already know, now you will have to find a way to connect the new information to the various points with such palace.

This leads us into the real nuts and bolts of the memory improvement system. Some people interested in this subject will want to know what they have to do after they have decided upon what journey to use, and what information they want to remember. Well, the answer depends upon how you are prepared to code the information and why you chose to code it the way you did. I told you earlier that the technique that I chose to use and have written this book about, is called the **Dominic Mnemonic or Dominic System**. (again I do not claim ownership of this particular method as the credit entirely goes to him, and not myself) However, before you start to believe that there is only one method out there for everybody in the memory world, let me open your eyes just a little bit to the other system that is also used just as frequently as this one.

The most common and oldest mnemonic system that is used in the field of memorization is referred to as the **Major Mnemonic**. Just to give you a little history lesson, the major mnemonic is a system where the person works by converting numbers into consonant sounds, then back into words by adding vowels in between. As you remember from grade school, vowels are the letters (**A, E, I, O, U**). This is referred to as the fill-in, or the information that you fill-in for the number that you are memorizing in order to make it an actual word. In this system, you will have to be able to vocally pronounce certain sounds or words and be able to recall the sounds acoustically in your memory so that you can create mental images. In the table below, the consonant sounds are listed however you will more than likely have to try to pronounce the various sounds over and over again in order to become familiar with how it feels to say them to yourself. Each numeral is associated with one or more consonants so that you have more than one choice. Vowels and the consonants *w, h,* and *y* are ignored for this purpose.

The Major Mnemonic system is organized like this, as I have included a table below to outline what the system looks likes.

Numeral	Sounds	Commonly associated letters
0	/s/, /z/	s, soft *c*, z, *x* (in *xylophone*)
1	/t/, /d/	t, d
2	/n/	N
3	/m/	M
4	/r/	r, *l* (in *colonel*)
5	/l/	L
6	/ch/, /g/ /sh/,	ch (in *cheese* and *chef*), j, soft g, sh, c (in *cello* and *special*), and *vision*), sc (in *fascist*), sch (in *schwa* and *eschew*)
7	/k/, /g/	k, hard c, q, ch (in *loch*), hard g
8	/f/, /v/	f, ph (in *phone*), v, gh (in *laugh*)
9	/p/, /b/	p, b, gh (in *cough*)

As you can see, each number is connected to a certain set of sounds and pronunciations, as well as tongue positions. In regards to this technique, the most important to remember is the actual phonetic sound that is made by the word. That is to say, it is the consonant sounds that matter most in this technique, not the actual spelling of the word. Like I said, you will have to probably write down different words for different combinations of letters that sound easy enough for you to not only pronounce, but also to visually imagine in your head. Therefore, a word like *"action"* would look (or sound) like the number *762*, as you can see from the future phonetic spelling (/k/-/sh/-/n/), not *712* (*k-t-n*). Double letters are disregarded when they are not pronounced separately, such as the word *muddy* sounds like *31* (/m/-/d/), not *311*, however the word *midday* would be like *311* (/m/-/d/-/d). This takes some time and practice in order to learn, it is the most complicated and advanced mnemonic learning system out there, however it has been proven to be extremely effective in memorizing number and letters and cards at almost supernatural speeds.

In this system, what we are really doing is trying to convert numbers to either letters or sounds. For most of us, this seems like an odd thing to do. We all grew up learning the alphabet as children as well as our numbers. Now, here we are trying to actually connect both systems of learning to each other. Well, before you assume that I am teaching you an alien language, let me start by explaining to you what is considered to be the core elements of memory learning. In order to learn something new, we have to know what exactly the information itself is really made out of. For example, when looking through computer programming codes and information, you are more than likely to see lots of binary codes and schematic frequencies. While this may sound like unfamiliar to most of us, this particular information is virtually the "alphabet" or the "core elements" of what makes up most computer programming materials. Thousands and thousands of codes could be written in various different ways in order to make the computer do various unexpected and unprecedented things.

However, before you start getting confused again (pretty sure by now you are feeling overwhelmed between talk of journeys and codes), I just want to reiterate that, although I am familiar with this particular type of mnemonic system, my main goal here in this book is to teach you a different yet similar system of memory. All I wanted to do was *introduce* you to the Major Mnemonic system, whether or not you chose to use it is based upon your preference.

I should point out that the main difference between the Dominic system and the major system is the assignment of *sounds and letters* to actually physical digits. The Dominic system is actually a letter-based abbreviation system where the letters comprise the initials of someone's name, while the major system is typically used as a phonetic-based consonant sounding system for objects, animals, persons, or even words. In other words, using the Dominic system, one could create words or images for numbers or cards using initials or abbreviations to stand for something dimensional in their minds rather than remembering corresponding sounds for such purposes. (you will see this come up in a later chapter soon)

The same infinite dexterity of the sounds of the alphabet is the same reason why many people enjoy listening to music so much. Just to refresh your memory, the actual notes that have used in music for the last ten centuries are the following: **A, B, C, D, E, F and G**. Think about it, there are only seven actual note sounds that have been deciphered by the human ear, some of them being sharp and others being flat. Sometimes the notes are long, sometimes they are short, and there are also all sorts of variously different combinations of how the notes can be connected to each other. Yet, when you look back at it all, even though there are only seven actual different actual notes, the possibilities of creating variously different forms and styles of music are simply endless.

Hundreds and thousands of pieces of music, ranging from classical to modern day hip hop, all are built from the same simple seven different individual notes. Now, just try to imagine what knowing 26 different letters or 100 different numbers can do for you in this new age of 21st century information overload. (we will explore this topic in a later chapter) Basically, everything that you will ever read through in life is made up of either the letters of the alphabet or the number 0-9. To have different codes for each integer or letter would you give unpredicted power over how to organize, categorize and eventually memorize any piece of information put before you.

In going back on the subject of the major system, in this memory system, the _sounds_ of T + L are assigned to the number 15, and then the person would have to find a word that has the same sounds as the first two consonants. Mnemonic images such as things like "tiles" or "toolbox" could be assigned under the major system using the number 15. In the Dominic system, the number 15 would actually stand for the letters **A** and **E**, and these letters could be used as the initials of someone's name—for example, Albert Einstein. Albert Einstein would then be given a **characteristic action**, such as "writing on a blackboard". Each two-digit number between 00 and 99 would have its own corresponding and associated "person" as well as distinctive action. The idea behind this is to sit down and make up a list of at least **100 different famous or fictional people** (*your future 100 character images as I will refer to by this name in later chapters*) whose initials correspond to the related numbers associated with those initials.

You will be asked to do this again in a later chapter for your next homework assignment. Each person, or character you create, must be different and unique from the previous one, meaning that each "character" needs to have his or her own trademark or distinguishing characteristic that sets them apart from all others. In this instance, the person using the Dominic system would only have to write out a list for each number from 00-99, and determine what letters correspond to each set of numbers, and then later decide upon a name for each person or character whose initials match that related set of letters. The actual chart or legend (if you are familiar with maps), is included below in order to help you the reader to understand how the Dominic system is organized.

Number	1	2	3	4	5	6	7	8	9	0
Letter	A	B	C	D	E	S	G	H	N	O

At first, this system seems to make sense when you count from the numbers 0-5, as we all are very familiar with the alphabet. For instance, O can look or be associated with the number 0. The letter A is the first letter of the alphabet, corresponding to the number 1, the letter B is associated with two, and so on. However, when we get to 6, the corresponding letter turns out to be the letter S. And for the number 9, the corresponding letter happens to be the letter N. For many of us, this can stop us dead in our tracks, as we begin to mentally go over the alphabet in our heads (remember the alphabet song) and realize that the sixth letter of the alphabet turns out to be the letter F, and the ninth letter happens to be I. For this formula, the word "**six**" actually starts with the letter **S**, and the word "**nine**" actually starts with the letter **N**. The reason we chose to do this is because for most people, it seems to be far easier and straightforward to imagine various characters and caricatures using only the associated letters as described. However, if you chose to create your own method of memory training, and wish to use the letters F and N, then please be my guest. The best thing about this method of memory training is that there is no real right or wrong way to correspond letters and numbers. It is entirely within the discretion of the user to determine what connections and associations that person choses to use, as long as such system makes sense to the individual person's needs.

In order to perform the encoding of numbers to letters correctly, each digit (0-9 or 00-99) needs to be linked to or associated with a letter using the table marked previously. These letters then become the initials of the person or character representing that number. Once the coding for a pair of digits is in place, a future linkage of digits can be changed into a story, by first encoding one pair of digits as a **person**, and then another pair of digits to resemble an **action** or **object**, and then chaining this person and action or object together in a small story. (we call this the **PAO system of memorization**) The first object to remember would be in the viewer's internal field of vision on their left-hand side or pictured as occurring on the far-left side of the particular memory location (loci) they are using. Then the second object would be remembered in the viewer's right-hand side, or just right next to the first object. This process itself is commonly referred to as "**setting the scene**".

I know all of this does not sound easy to understand. Try to imagine an actor on a stage, reciting Shakespeare to the crowded audience. You are in the front row watching this person perform. Try to picture such person standing on the far-left side of the stage from your vantage point. This "person" is gesturing sideways with their arm, and then talking to a fictional object on the right side of the stage, and this object represents something to the actor. In this instance, you could substitute a set of numbers to represent the person, and then another set of numbers to represent the <u>action of talking</u>, and another set of numbers to represent the <u>fictional object</u>.

As we have normally been trained to read a sentence starting from left to right, the Shakespearian actor is set to the far left of the scene as he represents the first item to be memorized, and the actor's arm is pointing to the next object on his right, which would be the second piece of information to remember, and so on. By doing this, you are effectively "**linking**" one character or object to another character or object. (this is called the **link or chain method**, which I will explore in a different chapter) Just imagine that by doing this imagery stage setting, you could possibly remember up to 6 numbers by just visually "<u>setting the scene</u>" of this one small imaginary make believe performance right in front of you.

Let's try examining one brief example of numbers memory for now to see how this system works. For example, one might remember the number 2739 as follows: First the number 27 would be encoded as **BG,** and then the initials could possibly be associated with someone famous, such as scientist Bill Gates. Then the number 39 would be encoded as **CN** and then the initials could correspond to someone else famous, such as actor Chuck Norris. As many of you hopefully remember (remember I was a child of the 80's), Bill Gates was the pioneering scientist who helped up to discover the PC computer and the first to create the Internet. So, the best image to conjure up would probably be a rich, scientific looking person (remember you don't have to remember Bill's exact features) sitting at a lap-top computer.

In addition, let's hope that you also remember who Chuck Norris is, the famous action star of the 1980's who was well known for his martial arts abilities. You don't have to remember exactly what Chuck Norris looks like, but to remember his martial arts abilities would be a good enough idea for now. So, using the first two digits as a person and the second two as an action, one could create the image of Bill Gates delivering a roundhouse kick to something in the room on his right side. In addition, the reverse number 3927 might be converted into the image of Chuck Norris sitting down at a computer, writing some type of software program. Try to visualize either scenario in your head as graphically as possibly, trying to imagine what you would think or feel if you were to encounter such a demonstration in real life.

In order to give you a classical definition of what you have just imagined, this is referred to in the memory business as **PAO**, or person-action-object system. It just seems to make sense in terms of the laws of physics or cause and effects. Normally, a person would engage in some type of action that would have an effect on another person or object next to them. This domino (or Dominic) effect of one thing affecting another is the gold standard for making memories stick or link together. We are all aware that there is such a thing known as gravity, so think of it as what goes up will always came back. Or, if you want to get more technical, every action has an equal or opposite reaction. This lets your mind always realize that the first item in a list of other items ultimately has an effect on the rest of the items. So, as you realize it, the link method and the PAO method seem to go hand in hand (or in this case, link to link, haha).

This phenomenon also helps in remembering long strings of numbers, as long as such numbers are imagined as occurring at variously different location points throughout a person's memory journeys. Longer numbers then become stories, which can be connected to each other in different way. The longer number 27396339, for example, could first be **chunked** in half, so that it looks like 2739 6339, and then later converted into BGCN SCCN. Using the "set the scene" procedure, if the individual can associate Santa Claus (63) with SC, then the number 2739 would represent Bill Gates (27) jumping up and giving a roundhouse kick (39) to Santa Clause (63), who is standing on the right side of the scene. Santa Clause then falls down and then gets back up and proceeds to give a roundhouse kick (39) right back to Bill Gates, who is on the left. All in all, this scene sounds rather odd and frightening to say the least, but don't worry, that is a good thing if you want to really remember things correctly. Now, try to imagine something like this happening in one of the rooms of your memory palace, you might experience a barrage of emotions just seeing this. But all in all, this makes the number not only easier to remember, but also a little bit fun and humorous to think of.

Also, not to surprise you too much at this point, but it would not be a bad idea to see if you can remember the information not just forwards, but also backwards as well (oh my god, for real!!!). Yes, this may seem crazy and ridiculous, but it is also helpful in allowing information to sink into your brain longer and stronger for better recall. Ever hear that expression "the back of my hand", well it does not just mean the opposite side of one's outer limbs. What it really means, in the memory world, is that if you know something so well then you should be able to recite it both forwards and backwards. Ever tried to remember your birth date or Social Security number in reverse, notice how different it feels to say it out loud as such. Also, by remembering information both forwards and backwards, it give you the chance to go over your information more than once so that you have rehearsed it more often, thereby giving you better memory.

In order to do these correctly, let's try to use one of the previous examples of 27396339, the one with Bill Gates on the left giving a karate kick to Santa Claus on the right, who then gets up and returns the favor back to him. In order to recall this information in reverse, instead of reading from left to right, we need to start **reading from right to left**. This would make the number look like 93369372 In this case; you would first have to recall the very last person or action that occurred in the sequence (karate kick- 39). Therefore, you would then recall that number as **93**, as the numbers are now reversed from 39. Then you would move onto the next item going from right to left (Santa Clause- 63). This would translate to **36 or CS**, as the numbers are reversed again. This process takes a little bit longer than memorizing them forwards. However, once you have recalled something going from start to finish, it is always best to review it as least one time going from finish to start. This way, the information has been learned in two different orders, and is therefore becomes more engrained into your brain and harder to forget. If you feel like it, give this number a try and see how it goes. Remember, imagination and associations are the keys to effectively setting the stage.

CHAPTER 4

How to use Dominic System (getting started) (link method, substitution) (creating journeys)

Wow, at this point in the book, you must be wondering about how to get started using the Dominic system and what steps are needed to ensure success. Well, don't be too worried, I will give you some handouts later that you can use in order to better organize your information and start the process of creating not only your own memory journeys (this can be a sweet trip down memory lane for most of us), but also your own mnemonic code system as well. The latter part takes some time and effort as you will need to create various codes to correspond to the related numbers that you plan on using. There are some websites on the Internet that you could use to look for some ideas about what characters or persons would be best suited for each pair of numbers. However, like I said earlier, there really is no right or wrong way to do this, as long as you make sure that the initials for each set of numbers corresponds correctly according to either the Dominic System scale or your own individual scale, whichever you are choosing to use. First, let's get started on a little memory homework assignment that can be used for all of your future memorization achievements.

Below is a scale that I created that helped me out when it came for me to try to come up with **100 different characters or persons** that I could use as references for my various codes or numbers. The columns are listed in a way that makes it easier for the person to organize their materials and to see how each set of numbers can be associated or linked to each pair of letters. The reference guide is listed below as follows:

NUMBER	INITIALS	NAME (person or character)	ACTION (what action most relates to them)	OBJECT (what object most relates to them)
00	OO	Whoever/ whatever	Action or sequence	Object or item
01	OA	Whoever/ whatever	Action or sequence	Object or item
02	OB	Whoever/ whatever	Action or sequence	Object or item
03	OC	Whoever/ whatever	Action or sequence	Object or item
04	OD	Whoever/ whatever	Action or sequence	Object or item
05	OE	Whoever/ whatever	Action or sequence	Object or item
06-100	Same as before Using Dominic Codes	Same	same	same

Also, if you ever wanted to memorize just single digits or numbers, simply just use the Dominic systems already mentioned and then try to create different images for each individual number. For example, in the Dominic System, the number **01** is equal to **A**. So, I could think of something special in my life that has the letter A in it, such as an apple. For the number **02**, the equivalent better for such number is **B**, so I could also think of something else in my life that also starts with the letter B, such as a banana. You can easily think of a few other images to correspond to the remaining numbers between 0-9 in your own spare time. By doing this, you can make room for the possibility of either having to memorize an odd amount of information, or just simply memorize numbers one digit at a time (though this may take longer, some people are okay with such method).

As they say in any battle, the only way to truly win a fight is with the strength of its troops. Here and now, I am going to give you your **first real assignment** in regards to preparing yourself for the battle of memory. In order to do this, you will need to have a "**company**" (military jargon aside) of your own creation. Earlier I spoke to you about that when using the Dominic System, it would be necessary to have characters or persons assigned to each number between 00 and 99. By this I mean, you will need to come up with **exactly 100 different characters or images** that you can think of that relate to the corresponding letter codes for each number (***this will be the single most important assignment to complete before you move on with this book, so please take your time and work on this first***). In order to do this correctly, you will have to create a numbered list going from 00-99, using the same format and organization as I have previously mentioned.

Remember, you can use the numerical coding system prescribed by Dominic O Brien, or your own personal scale, just make sure you write it down somewhere on the page to make sure you don't get it mixed up later. This process will take some time; don't be in a hurry to get the list done too quickly. The best advice I can give you is to simply go with what us in the memory world refer to as "**inner instinct**". That is to say, when you first write down the letter initials that are associated to its corresponding number, ask yourself what is the very first thing you think of when you see or hear the letters. It has to be something that takes less than a few seconds to come to your mind, something that feels natural or just simply makes sense to you. Always trust your instincts, as these things often take the least amount of mental energy to create. If the image is not too easy to conjure up, simply try to think of something else that is reasonably easy to picture, and that takes little to no effort. I have enclosed a reference chart for your convenience.

EXAMPLE OF NUMBER CODING CHART FOR DOMINIC SYSTEM:

NUMBERS	LETTERS	NUMBERS	LETTERS
00	OO	51	EA
01	OA	52	EB
02	OB	53	EC
03	OC	54	ED
04	OD	55	EE
05	OE	56	ES
06	OS	57	EG
07	OG	58	EH
08	OH	59	EN
09	ON	60	SO
10	AO	61	SA
11	AA	62	SB
12	AB	63	SC
13	AC	64	SD
14	AD	65	SE
15	AE	66	SS
16	AS	67	SG
17	AG	68	SH
18	AH	69	SN
19	AN	70	GO
20	BO	71	GA
21	BA	72	GB
22	BB	73	GC
23	BC	74	GD
24	BD	75	GE
25	BE	76	GS
26	BS	77	GG
27	BG	78	GH
28	BH	79	GN
29	BN	80	HO

30	CO	81	HA
31	CA	82	HB
32	CB	83	HC
33	CC	84	HD
34	CD	85	HE
35	CE	86	HS
36	CS	87	HG
37	CG	88	HH
38	CH	89	HN
39	CN	90	NO
40	DO	91	NA
41	DA	92	NB
42	DB	93	NC
43	DC	94	ND
44	DD	95	NE
45	DE	96	NS
46	DS	97	NG
47	DG	98	NH
48	DH	99	NN
49	DN		
50	EO		

For this scale, when I see the number **02**, I already think of the letters **OB**. Here, I "instinctively" think of Obi Wan Kenobi from Star Wars (I am a big science fiction fan, don't knock it). Anyway, when I say the name Obi Wan, it even sounds like I am saying the letters OB, hence it is the first thing that comes to mind. However, this does not always work for every single combination of letters. You will have to sometimes not go with your instincts for certain letters, as some combinations of letters are difficult to imagine any related characters for. So please use your best judgment and decide for yourself what character or person you are most comfortable with using for each combination of letters. Try to make sure that each character is someone different or unique from the others. The more closely similar two characters are, the greater the chance that when you want to start memorizing long strings of information, you might confuse one combination of characters for another. Also, don't forget that the more outrageous or unique the character you think of is, the better the chance you will never forget it or confuse it with anything else.

So, since I mentioned earlier that I am a big Star Wars fan, this is the reason why the number 02 is related to the letter **OB**, and OB is related to Obe Wan. Also, the number **86** is related to Han Solo. The number **8** is related to the letter **H**, and the number **6** is related to the letter **S**, hence HS or Han Solo. Since they are both characters in the same franchise, I have to make sure that I differentiate between the two of them so that when the time comes for me to memorize 8602 or 0286; I have at least one distinctive feature for each one of them. The number 8602 would be Han Solo brandishing a Light Saber (as you know from the movies, that he never actually touched one), and the number 0286 would Obe Wan piloting the Millennium Falcon, as you know that he never actually flew the ship. Either way, I can easily see each figure as being separate and unique from each other, even though they are both similar as being from the same franchise. As Yoda would say, "the force is strong with you, young Jedi".

Speaking of the force being strong with you, let me help you to remember another famous scene from my beloved Star Wars odyssey that illustrates my next point. There is a scene from the movie "The Empire Strikes Back", during which Yoda is training Luke Skywalker in the art of using the force. Suddenly one of the ships that Luke was previously using suddenly sinks into a pond, and is submersed in water. Luke looks on helplessly, thinking that he does not have the strength or the ability to pull such ship out of the water.

He feels that the task if much more difficult to accomplish as opposed to lifting rocks in the air by using the Force. Yoda looks at him and says "it is no different, only different in your mind; you must unlearn what you have learned". Initially afraid of failure, Luke states that he will at least try to relocate the ship. However, Yoda exclaims, "No, there is do or do not, there is no try". At first, Luke does try hard to lift the submerged ship from its watery grave, but the amount of weight seems just too much for him. As he walks away from the pond with his head down in defeat, and feeling sorry for himself, Yoda quietly closes his eyes, concentrates hard, gently moves his hands, and then proceed to gradually lift the entire ship out of the water and carefully place it on the safe and dry shore area. Luke is so amazed and perplexed by this incredible act of cognitive strength that he exclaims "I can't believe it". Yoda then simply looks at him and says "that is why you fail".

On that wise philosophical note, I think it would be important to explain to you about the **power of imagination** and how it helps to achieve an ultimate memory. Most of us are familiar with old fables and myths such as Santa Claus, the Bogeyman, the Tooth Fairy and the Easter Bunny. And these characters were much easier to create during our early imaginative childhood years. Well, don't worry, even back in those days, having an imagination as strong as that was the key to remembering things much more clearly than we do today as adults. It seems as though every child under the age of 6 has more eidetic memory than most adults do.

As times goes on, the ability to conjure up such ridiculous images seems to fade more and more from our adult minds, as we are constantly inundated with the harsh realities of life, and less with the carefree and relaxed feelings of early childhood fantasy. The important point to remember here is that the stronger or more powerful you make your imagination is, the better you will be able to recall something through memory. Hence, it is no different in terms of the actual amount of information to remember, it is only different in your mind as far as how graphic you make the images. (remember the way of the Jedi, haha)

Think of it like this, would you be better able to remember something that seemed boring and familiar, or something that was **outlandish** and **unexpected**. Chances are, you would be better able to remember the latter item as opposed to the first one. (that is the reason for the previous story of the elephant with the ice cream)The reason for this is that we only remember the good and bad days of our lives, never the boring days in between. For this reason, you will need to be able to use your imagination to make sure that your future characters are engaged in wild and graphically crazy activities in order to visualize them longer and clearly. For example, when trying to recall the number 8602 (Han Solo with the light saber), instead of just pretending that Han Solo is holding a light saber, I could try to visualize him wildly swinging the light saber and then accidentally hurting his foot. (that would hurt a lot, ouch)

As well, when I try to recall 0286, I could try to imagine Obe Won Kenobi trying to fly the Millennium Falcon by using the force to move the controls without using his hands, as opposed to him sitting down at the control seat like a normal pilot. As you can see, both images are much more unusual and out of the ordinary as opposed to the previous scenario for such character. So, please try to understand about the power of your imagination, and just how it determines how well your memory truly can be.

The phrase I chose to use to remember my images is like this: **POP**. This stands for two things, first it stands for **p**erson, **o**bject or **p**lace. Second, it actually means the word **POP**. (imagine popcorn bursting up in your face) When you try to come up with your 100 different images or characters, it is important to have your **POP (person, object, or place)** literally POP right in front of your face through the inner senses of your mind. This means that you have to try to imagine things happening amongst your imaginary characters that could never truly or really happen either in your imagination or the real world. As difficult as this seems, it allows you to somehow abandon abstract reasoning and logical thought, and instead delve deep into the world of creative and illustrative cognitive thinking. You will need to create your own weird "stories" for each group of characters, as it will be easier for you to remember them if they are engaged in some type of activity or with some type of object that seems out of place for them.

Once you finally get done with your list of 100 characters, actions and associated objects, the next and most important step would be to actually make sure you have set up your multiple memory journeys, or simply your chalk boards for remembering things. The reason why I chose to use the word "**chalk board**" (again, I am a child of the 80's and 90's, we did not always have smart boards then), is because when you actually get done using your memory palace to store information, that information will only remain safe in such location until you chose to use it again for another purpose. The way it works is like this, when you actively chose to associate information into one of your memory palaces and you rehearse it over and over again, it will stay there for a definitive period of time. However, you will not be able to associate any other or new information into that palace at that time, or else some of what you remember will become "clouded over" or erased by the new information. At this point, you will probably get confused between new information you are memorizing and more recent information that you were thinking about earlier.

Imagine a chalk board with lots of information written down on it. Once the teacher is done writing it down, the only way for he or she to write down any other information is to either get a new board (another memory journey) or to erase everything and start again. If you chose to use the same memory palace over and over repeatedly, you could start getting confused later on, and some information may end up being linked or crossed over with old information, much like an eraser stain needs some time to disappear. The reason why I am offering this advice to you today is because, in the following exercise, you will need to created multiple or numerous memory palaces so that you have enough room and space to store as much information as you would like so that you are not limited to just one or two chalkboards. (by the way, as my mother was a teacher, so I always remember the good old days of using a chalk board during class)

However, one thing we did not talk about earlier in our discussion, was the question of how does one actually "walk" through a memory palace in the first place, without really having to physically walk at all. This will be the part of our discussion where you get the chance to reminisce about every single place that you have ever lived in, visited, spent time, or had random experiences in during the course of your life. As I said earlier, places that you currently or recently have seen will be fresh in your mind, older places might be harder to visualize.

Don't worry about looking up any information about the layout of the place, just use your best judgment as far as how you remembered the place to look, nobody will be able to read your mind or correct your mistakes. With regards to how to actually set up a memory palace, there are two main steps that I use in order to outline the information accurately. First, draw or sketch a picture of the outline of the house or residence that you want to remember. Use squares, rectangles, symbols for stairs, windows, door, and related furniture. Here is a description of what the master bedroom in my house would look like from my perspective if I were to enter it through the door.

Try to picture yourself walking through the door of my bedroom and the first thing you see in front of you is my new master bed. Right behind that is the dresser that my wife uses for some of her clothes and jewelry. To the left of that dresser are the main windows and the AC unit for the room. To the left of that in the corner, is the TV stand and our TV. Also to the left of this is my wife's other dresser and cabinet. Then the exit closet door to get to our hidden closet (we call it Narnia, from the Witch and the Wardrobe book, again children of the 80's) And finally, you will find yourself at my long clothes dresser, before returning to the main door of the room.

If you have noticed, I have taken you on a small journey through one of my rooms, going in a specific direction. Like many of us that have ever used a watch or seen a clock, we are all too familiar with the expressions "**clockwise" and "counter clock wise**". In this instance, I took you "counter clock wise" through my room, first arriving at the door or entrance way. Then looking straight ahead and seeing the bed, then looking behind it and seeing my wife's dresser. And then proceed to go to the left each time, or counter-clockwise, so that you could run into each and every major item in my one bedroom.

Now that you have "walked" through your first ever memory palace, the next step would be to try to go through it again at least a few times, both forward and backward. However, once you are finished you will be using your "powers of imagination" to place various items at different locations along the same path of the journey. If you were starting out at the entrance door to my bedroom, imagine that there one of your future characters or images are standing in the doorway, blocking you from entering. Then as you push past such image and keep moving, you will get to the master bed, where you will encounter another one of your characters or images doing something on the bed. And then you will proceed past this and move onto my wife's dresser, where you will notice another one of your characters or images engaged in some action involving the jewelry.

By placing these images at various places around the room that you are intimately familiar with, and giving them associated actions for each location that you can readily identify, you could easily imagine yourself going from place to place in such room, visualizing each new character or image when you arrive at each new location, before moving onto to the next one. It will feel as if you are walking through a fun house of sorts, encountering different scenarios wherever you turn.

Here is a little <u>homework assignment</u> to help get you more acquainted with the idea of a memory palace. Next time you walk into a room of a building that you are familiar with, first notice the point of view or angle that you are seeing things when you first arrive at the entrance door. Either the door will be to the left or right-side entrance to a room. Try to make this your initial or "first" location in a room. After that, try to notice the next major thing about the room that attracts your eyes. This will be the "second" location in the room. It could be a piece of furniture, a picture, a window, or some other personal item. Then decide for yourself if you would like to "walk" through the room either clockwise or counter-clock wise.

Do this for each and every major or large object that falls within that path, and number each location until you eventually return back to the door you started at. Try to use the same turn of direction for each room you talk through in your journeys, it will make it easier to remember what items are coming first and second, as opposed to changing direction each time you get to another room. You can use the same philosophy when it comes to getting over to the next room, depending on how your palace rooms are connected to each other

If you read beneath this paragraph, you will notice another example of a memory palace. Below is the a detailed description of what my living room looks like by taking an imaginary trip through another memory palace. Try to imagine yourself starting out near my late Grandmother's TV set and VCR (I assure you there are no Beta Max devices to be found, haha). Just remember my previous advice about what direction you want to travel through the room and where you want to place your random images. Then, once you finally walk away from the TV, imagine yourself resting on my dark brown coach, with all my cats sleeping on it. Do the same thing here with regards to placing your images and deciding what direction to turn. Right next to that is our old coffee table with an assemble of candles and fragrances on it. Afterwards you can move over to my wife's tan recliner/easy chair and sit back and enjoy yourself. Then you move on and be careful not to touch our antique china set cabinet. As you take a turn who will see that you are looking out our window into the street, then stop by the gold lamp I got for my birthday. (I keep a lot of sentimental objects in my house; it helps me to remember them more)

Then you will come across our CD set and related CDs and DVDs, where we used to keep my stereo set. Then finally, you will see the area where I used to have a piano stand (gave it away years ago, but I still remember what it looks like). See yourself walking and turning through each location, asking yourself what point of view you would prefer to take to visualize every time you turned from one place to another. Sometimes, you will see the item as being right in front of you, other times you will see if from the side depending on how you angle your inner field of vision. Remember, this is your journey; the way that you walk through the house is entirely your decision, just make sure you don't get lost or forget where you left off, as this will cause your information to be misfiled when you go back and try to rehearse it.

Congratulations, you have just taken your first memory journey through someone else's house. Don't' worry, you are not invading my privacy (just call before you try to actually come over, haha). Now, do this for each and every house that you are either recently familiar with or places that you have not seen in many years. It could be friends, relatives, neighbors, coworkers, or just total strangers. As long as you have been in their house at least a few times, you should have a pretty good idea of the layout of most of the rooms. Remember the layout of the rooms compared to each other, decide where you want to start (usually this is going to be the farthest away point), and then proceed from room to room until you either leave the house or exit into another floor.

Make sure you count and keep track of each and every single location that catches your glimpse, including all doors, windows, furniture, hallways and staircases, as these will easily attract your eye. Then once you are confident that you are "traveled" through your memory palace well enough, use the following diagram and list to help you remember the travel spots that you are seen along the way. Do this for each and every memory palace you wish to create, if you need to, keep a notebook or a binder for such purposes and label each journey as a separate page. Include a physical diagram alone with the written list for each one. (this is an example of a Journey Journal, I will explain more in later chapters)

() TITLE OF MEMORY JOURNEY (ex, your house, apartment, work, etc)

Location #	Description of location (what the location actually is, looks like, and what it means)
1st	TV set (on my left hand side of vision)
2nd	Couch (as I turn and look directly at it)
3rd	Coffee table (as I turn right to walk away from couch)
4th	Easy chair (as I turn straight and look ahead)
5th	China cabinet (as I start to turn right and move forward)
6th	Windows (as I straighten up and start walking back to door)
7th	Lamp (in my left field of vision)
8th	Stereo set (as I look toward the door)
9th	Piano set (leaving the room)
10th	Same as before
11th	Same as before
12th	Same as before
13th	Same as before
14th	Same as before

Chapter 5

Let's see how your memory feels now

Hello again, welcome back to the wonderful world of memory improvement. At this point, hopefully you have taken the time to make up a list of at least **100 different major characters** or persons of interest that correspond to the related numerals for their initials (i.e. 15= AE or Albert Einstein, 27= BG or Bill Gates, etc). And perhaps you have had some time to go back down memory lane and think about creating at least several memory palaces or journeys of your own, regardless of whether they come from places that you have lived or other related residences. It is a good idea to have at least ten to twenty separate memory palaces, each with at least 15-30 different locations for each one. And you should probably both draw sketches of them or at least write out the lists of the descriptions of the various locations for each palace. At this point, you already have all the necessary tools and ingredients needed to master your memory. Congratulations, you have now just stepped through the looking glass of your brain and have entered an entirely new dimension of thinking.

Now, the only thing left to do is to *CHALLENGE YOURSELF.* (don't think I would ever forget about the introductory exercise that we all started out with at the beginning). As you probably recall, I did ask you to look at three different lists of information to memorize within a certain period of time. For now, we are only going to concentrate on just the <u>first list of numbers</u> (I still have to give you a future lesson on both card memory and word memory in later chapters, so we will stick with numbers for now). Don't worry, I believe that you are more prepared now that you were before. So, this time, I want you to get out two pieces of paper like before, as well as a pencil and a stopwatch. Write down all of the numbers as you did previously on the first exercise. Make sure you write the number from left to write in a long-stretched line on your paper, giving some space between the numbers. You will not need to cover the answers for the other columns as you will only be focusing on one subject for now, which is numbers. After you have written down all of the numbers accurately, flip the page over and don't look at it.

When you are ready, decide which memory palace you would like to use for this one. Take a few minutes and go through such palace thoroughly, stopping at each location and keeping count of which location is first, second and so on. Then go back and rehearse all of your codes for the numbers 00-99, making sure that you individually pay attention to each number and remember either the person or the character that you associated with such number. Try to give yourself a few seconds for each number, say the number out loud and then the name of the person or character that is assigned for each number. Do this by closing your eyes and visualizing what he or she looks like and what object is synonymous with him or her. Make sure you are able to visually "see" each character in your mind so that each person is clearly visible for the next exercise.

Once you feel that you are completely confident about your particular memory journey and the number codes from 00-99, then flip the page back over, start your stop clock, read the numbers from left to right, and see how well you do this time. (**trust me, you are about to have your first lightbulb or ah-ha moment**). Give yourself 5 minutes for the memorization and five minutes for the recall. Once your initial five minutes for memorization are up, turn your page over again so that you cannot see the numbers that you wrote at the beginning. Take out your blank answer sheet form. Proceed to write out as many of the numbers as you remember in the same order. Once you are done, look at both sheets of paper as well as your stopwatch. See how many numbers you got correct, and also see how long it took for you to get through this exercise. Make sure to mark down your time. After all of this, look at the answer sheet from this exercise and compare it to the paper from your first exercise at the beginning of the book. Notice the differences in scores and test timing. (let's see how much better you did this time)

(Complete the exercise first before you move onto the next paragraph)

Well, it is my hope that either you demonstrated a perfect recall of all the numerical material, or at the very least, you possibly doubled your previous score. Either way, take a moment and let it all sink into your head. Ask yourself, *how do you feel knowing that you have just achieved something you never thought humanly possible like that?* You must be scratching your head or looking up into the sky wondering, how did I just do that? For those of us who think that this was just some random act of luck or that something in the original numbers has changed, let me confess something important to you all. The numbers that were given to you were chosen <u>specifically in order to prove to you</u> that you already knew the images that were associated with such numbers in the first place. (Surprise, bet you didn't see that easy one coming, did you?)

If you look back at the sequence, the first numbers were 247365. A better way to read this sequence is 24/7 and 365/1. Does this look familiar to you now? 24/7 stands for 24 hours a day, seven days a week. 365/1 stands for 365 days a year. How about the next group of number? 911742019 can actually translated to mean 9/11, 7/4, 2019. In other words, 9/11 refers to the World Trade Center, 7/4 refers to July 4th and 2019 was the year that I sat down and started writing this book. I bet that the images of each combination are just jumping out of your head right now. Do you see how easy some of the images are just because you have decided that there is always a certain type of a coding, organization and chunking that can be applied to any and all material.

I bet now you are probably thinking that this exercise was harder than it should have been. Well, the truth is yes, it was meant to be harder than it should have been. There might be some of you out there that were able to catch some of the other combinations of numbers and knew what they stood for. But for now, realize that you now have two different ways of memorizing numbers as opposed to your original first style. At this point, you now have multiple styles of learning and comprehension.

Don't worry; it does not matter whether you chose to use the Dominic System alone to remember these numbers, or if you try to use this new revelation of images in conjunction with the Dominic System. If you try to combine the two, it makes the memory system so much more effective to use, as you are trying to remember information in two different ways, making the information even more difficult to forget. The point is, all you need to really do is make the information meaningful and explanatory in your head, seeing each group of numbers as having some personal or intimate meaning to you. And if you can't do that, use the Dominic System to illustrate the 100 images that you already have created, and make a wild and crazy story out of all combinations of numbers characters.

Now then, why don't we try to actually memorize some numbers or combinations of numbers in a different pattern to see how well you actually know the Dominic System, and see how confident you feel in using your memory palaces. Do you remember earlier what I said about "setting the scene" when it comes to creating images as if they were on a stage in front of you? In this instance, the first item would be on the left and the next being on the right. Well, now it is time to start organizing your organization skills. (sounds pretty much like OCD at this time point, huh).

Well, the reason why I suggest that we do this is because, your memory palace can serve not only as a filing cabinet for all of your information, but it can also be used as a map for locating specific information that you want to locate and pull out at a moment's notice. Ever seen a filing cabinet that was not arranged in ABC or numerical order? It can be quite overwhelming to the average onlooker, as it would take a long time to go through the entire thing until you find what you are looking for. What if there was a way for you to have specific locations set up in your memory palaces, so that you could locate specific types of information before you even get started? That would you make not only able to recall the information both forward and backward, but also to individually locate any one piece of information that you want at any given time, and know its location. Let's take a few minutes and see how it is done.

As you recall from my previous description, when you created your own memory palaces, you could either draw a picture of each room and location on a sheet of paper, or you could create a numerical list of all the different loci and points of reference. By doing either of these things, you now have the ability to organize your materials in a more realistic way. The next step is to actually know how much information you want to store at each location. Earlier, in the activity known as "setting the scene", you were told to imagine a character on the left side of a stage, pointing to someone or something else on the right side of the stage.

The first character represented the first 2 numbers, the other character or object represented the next 2 numbers. If you were to imagine such a scenario playing out at any one of your locations within your memory palace, you would have the ability to easily remember an average of at least 4 numbers for each location. The only thing you have to remember is to place the first item in your left field of vision and the other image in your right field of vision. (if you become really good at this, like myself, you could probably double that amount per each location if you have enough space). This allows you to always know that the amount of information that you can remember at each location will be 4, 6, or 8, depending on how many characters or images you put at each loci. It is best to always stick with the same number of characters for each location, as well as the same amount of numerical digits as well, so that you don't get bogged down by the math. (I always hated division growing up)

When I chose to memorize numbers, I am able to put 2 different characters in each location standing right next to each other, thereby allowing me to get 4 digits of numbers per location. And when I do this, I make up a short story or "play" for how all the characters and objects interact. This allows me to have better control of the mathematical calculations needed to recall where the 10th, 20th, or 30th digit would be located. All I have to do count each location as either being the first, second or third location, then just multiply that number by four, and this lets me know what group of numbers correspond to which location. For example, if I were to memorize 40 different numbers, that would take me at least 10 different locations to fit all of it in. If I needed to recall what the 27th number I memorized was, for example, I would realize that the first location could only be used for the first four numbers, and then the second location was to be used for the next four numbers and so on. (i.e. Location one (**#1-4**), location two (**#5-8**), location three (**#9-12**).

Therefore, it is easy to realize that the 27th number would be located in the 7th location in your memory palace, as this location could encompass the 25th to 28th digits in the sequence. In this order, the 27th number would be in the first initial of the second character or object on the right hand side of location 7. I have enclosed another chart underneath to show you have it is organized. Try using this as a reference guide for those of you who have already completed your palaces. It refers to the previous memory journey list that was used for my living room.

(#) TITLE OF MEMORY JOURNEY (ex, your house, apartment, work, etc)

Location #	Description of location (include what the location actually is and what it means)
1st	TV set (items #1-4)
2nd	Couch (items #5-8)
3rd	Coffee table (items #9-12)
4th	Easy chair (items #13-16)
5th	China set cabinet (items #17-20)
6th	window (items #21-24)
7th	Lamp (items #25-28)
8th	Stereo location (items #29-32)
9th	Piano (items #33-36)
10th	Door leading out (items #37-40)

Okay, are you ready for another challenge? (as if you haven't been challenged enough as it is). Well, I am going to give you two more challenges to complete, in different time sequences and with different recall patterns. I have included <u>two new lists of numbers</u>, this time from left to right, with some spacing in between digits to help you out. The first list has **40 numbers** in it, just a little more than the first challenge. The next list has **60 numbers** in it. You will need to cover up the second list while you are memorizing the first one, as you probably remember from the previous exercise at the beginning.

In addition, now that you know how to use mnemonic codes and have probably created 100 characters, please feel free to use a pencil or a pen to mark off or draw lines between certain amounts of information if it helps you to keep your place. You will also need two sheets of paper and a stopwatch. For **the first list**, you will have <u>only 4 minutes</u> to see how much information you can remember in that time period, and then <u>5 minutes</u> for recall. For the **second list**, you will have <u>6 minutes</u> to recall as much information as you can, as well as <u>5 minutes</u> for recall. (This adds up to 10 minutes total to remember 100 numbers in a row, think you can do it?) Give yourself <u>1 point</u> for each correct answer, and then add both scores and times for a grand total.

Now here is the tricky part, as I want to really test your memory strengths and abilities. After you are done with each, I want you to write down the memorized information both forwards and <u>backwards</u> during your recall. (Yes, that right, believe me it will be necessary for you to do this in future challenges.) You will recall from earlier chapters what I referred to as the "<u>back of my hand</u>". Well, now is your chance to see if you can not only recall either 100 numbers in just 10 minutes total, but to also see if you can also remember it in reverse order as well.

When you are done with this exercise, I would like for you to write out the first list of numbers in **correct** order (beginning to end). And then for the second and larger list, I would like for you to recall it back in **reverse** order (end to beginning). In order to make sure that you are correct, you could check off each number one at a time during recall to see if you are making progress. So for instance, if the last number is a 9 according to the list, you would try to write down 9 as your first number at the top of your list, and then carefully check to see if you are getting each one right by going down the list. Believe me folks, if you could be able to do this, it would give you a mental ability you never thought possible, as now you are able to recall information faster, more accurately and in different order. The lists of the numbers are as follows: Good luck.

(complete the exercise)

LIST 1:

5 9 8 4 6 8 5 2 3 5 7 4 5 8 4 6 2 1 5 9 8 4 5 2 3 5 7 9 4 6 5 8 1 5 3 2 4 5 6 7

Total score=total time=

LIST 2:

7 6 9 8 1 6 4 8 5 9 3 2 4 6 8 8 5 4 2 1 2 1 9 6 3 5 7 4 6 6 5 6 2 8 4 9 6 3 6 3 8 7 9 9 5 9 5 7 4 6 8 5 4 4 2 4 1 8 6 9

Total score=total time=

Now for one more last training session on numbers, I would like to put your through final drill instruction for memory training (sir yes sir, Drill Sgt Dan). As part of your homework assignment, I would like for to practice using any of the previous 3 listed groups of numbers for future training exercises. You now have one list with 30 digits, one list with 40 digits and another list with 60 digits. In this instance, I would like for you to try to memorize just one list of numbers each day and try to time yourself to see how fast and accurate your recall is for now. Just try to remember them in correct order for now, not reverse order.

Hopefully you have several memory palaces ready to practice with, so you will have options to choose from and don't use the same palace over and over again (remember the whole lesson about the chalk board phenomenon). For the first day, only pick one list of numbers and nothing else, and just memorize that one list. The next day, chose another list of numbers and do the exact same thing. Hopefully, by the end of the week, you should be able to try to memorize each list at least twice if you are organized well enough. Continue doing this for exactly one week, try noticing how much faster your time is and how much better your scores are getting.

Look to determine what your strengths and weaknesses are with regards to certain images and with certain locations in various palaces. You will find that some images are harder to remember or picture than others, and that some locations are more difficult to store information than others. If needed, you could try to change some of your images if they are becoming too complex for you. You could also re-organize some of your memory palaces to make it easier to travel through them more quickly and efficiently. Don't forget to rehearse and go over your various codes from 00-99 before hand to make sure that you are still familiar with them. (You might believe it but it helps to practice this for a few minutes each morning, as you will likely forget some of your characters if you don't regularly practice.) You will be encouraged to keep drilling with this weekly chart for this and other related memory tasks, so as to help keep you practicing and practicing for weeks and even months to come. I have included a score sheet for you to use as part of your training "regimen", use this as a reference guide to note your progress and scores.

DAY EXERCISE	SCORE (PERCENT/ CORRECT)	TIME (MINUTES, SECOND)
FIRST DAY		
SECOND DAY		
THIRD DAY		
FOURTH DAY		
FIFTH DAY		
SIXTH DAY		
SEVENTH DAY		

AVERAGE SCORE=

AVERAGE TIME=

CHAPTER 6

What is in a word (word memory) (substitution method)

When I was as a child, I remember growing up in the Middletown school district. Back then, my mother was a teacher in the same school that I was also a student. During those young and formidable years, there were plenty of times when my other teachers would assign the class to remember a list of words, usually numbered from 1-20, each month for a regularly scheduled spelling test. I used to hate those tests, as I was always worried, not only about remembering the spelling of the words, but also the actual order of the words themselves. My mother would sit up with me and my brother each week and thoroughly go over each and every word and its spelling. Even though the class would go over the information repeatedly just before each test, it did not stop me from having regular bouts of test anxiety. If only there could have been some way that I could have been better able to memorize vocabulary words at that time, I might have gotten perfect scores on all my quizzes.

Well, perhaps we can try to get off of the subject of numbers for just a moment, and try to focus on something else that you were tested on earlier. The second list of information in your initial exercise was a list of <u>exactly 30 different vocabulary words</u> that were to be memorized in order in less than 5 minutes. Thankfully, for this particular type of memory experience, you don't have to worry too much about using your "numerical codes" or related letter combinations; however you might have to use them a little bit. And what makes this better for you, is the fact that all of the words that I gave you earlier were nouns, which means that they were persons, objects or places.

Nouns are usually the easiest thing to visualize as most of us have either personally seen these nouns or have the ability to possibly imagine what they would look like. You will still have to use your imagination again for this next chapter on memory. Refer back to the section that deals with <u>imagination power</u> (inner senses) which deals with trying to make your images stand out or seem wild and unruly in your mind. Also, you will definitely need to continue to organize your memory palaces more so that you only place a certain amount of information at each location. However, before you get too relaxed and confident, I have yet another surprise for you as I am prepared to teach you <u>two additional memory methods</u>. The methods that you are about to discover in this next section are **the link method, and the substitution method.**

What are you kidding me? How many more methods are there to learn at this point? That is exactly what I said when I first heard about these two new concepts. However, before you start to have any anxiety or panic like I first did when I read about these methods, just realize that you probably have already been using the methods since I first introduced you to the concepts of <u>symbol encoding</u> and <u>walking through memory palaces</u>. When you think about the word "**link**", it usually conjures to mind an image of either a chain or a rope that is able to connect or "**link**" two items together so that they are forever connected to each other. The <u>setting the scene sequence</u> that was explained earlier is the very same concept described here. In this instance, you will learn how best to make connections between any two unrelated and dissimilar entities or objects in such a way. This will allow your imagination and mental creativity to be exercised to the point of almost artificially creating your own hallucinations in your mind (the title of the book <u>shrink</u> is starting to make more sense now, isn't it).

First, let's start with the link method. As you probably remember from my "setting the stage" discussion, when you try to remember four numbers together, the first two numbers would constitute one person and the second two numbers would resemble the second person. Now, let's take the **link method** out for a spin in this situation, shall we? Look back at the original list of words that I gave you at the beginning of the book. Try to remember each of your 100 characters or persons that you created earlier. Go through the list from 0-99 and slowly call out each image and number until you are finished. Now, look at the list of the words that I gave you earlier in the introduction of the book. If you would like, you could rewrite the characters again with the numbers next to them on another sheet of paper.

Do you see what is happening here? You are about to try to link your initial characters for your numbers right next to the listed noun that you are trying to remember. For example, the number 27 is Bill Gates or BG, and the 27th word on the vocabulary list is "robot". Now try to imagine Bill Gates is on your left side, and he is fashioning together a robot. And that the robot turns out to be as vicious HAL-2000 machine. From this story, you have linked the number 27 with the 27th word on the list. At this point, it is almost impossible to not be able to remember the entire list of words from start to finish. As long as you are comfortable with your related 100 character images, and have some inkling of imagination in regards to vocabulary, you will have no problem doing this vocabulary assignment.

Now, for this exercise, I would like for you to write out the words as previously listed on another sheet of paper, this time numbered all the way down the page from 1 to 30. Get ready to get your stopwatch out again and prepare to time yourself. Again, you will have 5 minutes to memorize as many of the items on the page as possible. Once you are done memorizing, you will then flip the page over and write out as much information as you can recall on another page. Also, remember that spelling does count for this exercise as some items are singular and others items are plural. You will have 5 minutes for recalling all of the information. Once you are done, go back and check to see how well you did. Record your score and see if you have improved from your first test. Good luck. Oh and by the way, before you think that this is the only way to remember words, I have another important lesson for you to utilize once you are done with this exercise.

**(Complete the exercise, do not move onto
the next page until finished)**

Hopefully you made quite an improvement on your vocabulary memory this time around as opposed to your initial attempt. I hope that you can see how simple and effective the link method is when you are trying to recall the exact order and sequence of information, especially if you already have at least 100 different characters or persons that you can associate with each vocabulary word. Now, we will have another go at trying to use our memory palaces again, only this time we are going to try to memorize a whole new list of vocabulary words instead of numbers. Hopefully, you will not be completely burnt out by the numbers exercises from before that you have not yet already overused any of your memory palaces. Please take the time to try to think of new and improved memory palaces from other expeditions in your life, such as vacations, work places, other relatives' houses, libraries or shopping malls. This way, you will still have some variety in regards to what memory palaces you chose to use and how fresh and unfilled some of those palaces probably are.

However, before you start to think that this is the only way that you can memorize vocabulary words, let's try to go back to using our Memory Palace technique to try to recall some vocabulary words instead of using number correlations. If you would look at the initial list of vocabulary words, you will see that the first four words are as follows: calendar, office, flag and building. If you wanted to remember the first four words from the list using the Memory Palace technique, you could try to remember what the first location in your memory palace was, and then make up a story using the first four words listed previously. In this instance, you could visualize a large calendar on your left, which falls down and lands in an office garbage can. Next to this, you see a small flag that is mounted on top of a miniature building. By following this sequence, you can easily recall the first four words of the initial vocabulary list.

In addition, remember earlier when I talked to you about the setting the scene exercise? Well I did just ask you to remember 4 different items at each location in one of your memory palaces. Now, just try to realize that you are already able to remember all of your 100 image characters from the previous numerical exercise. Do you think that it would be possible to also connect each one of your 100 character images to the start of a chain for 4 separate words? Think about it like this. First, you need to determine what is your character for the number 01? (**OA**) My personal character for **OA** is a Boy Scout camp fire because the letters OA stand for Order of the Arrow, a secret fraternity in the Scouting program. (remember, I am an Eagle Scout, so be prepared).

Below you will see another list of vocabulary words for your convenience. And the first four words in this list are: *race car, hamburger, casket and marbles.* The image that I have connected for 01 or OA is a campfire. So I could try to imagine the first four words from the list like this: a <u>camp fire</u> sets off the flames and embers that ignite <u>a race car</u>, which someone decides to cook <u>hamburgers</u> on, and then flips one behind his back, where the burger lands in an <u>open casket</u>, where it is discovered that the casket is loaded with <u>marbles</u>. By doing this, I have linked all four of the first four words together; hopefully all of them can be stored together in just one room of one of your memory palaces if needed.

This is a rather odd scene, but in actuality, I just memorized the first 4 words by connecting them to my very first image character. I know that this might take some time, but just realize that if you were able to make up a 4 word item short story, and connect that story to each of the 100 separate number characters from your 100 image list. And then you were able to try to use lots of odd and creative visual images and place them in different rooms of your memory palace. You could eventually be capable of remembering at least 400 vocabulary words in just one sitting. That is the <u>average amount of actual words</u> that are printed on one sheet of paper in any adult's novel. I realize that most words in such novels also include verbs, pronouns, adjectives, etc. All I can say is that as long as you look at each word and decide for yourself what the word sounds or looks like just by using the <u>substitution method</u>, you could very well shock your friends and colleagues by mentally reading off each and every word on one single page of a book. (Talk about virtual reading, huh?)

But don't worry, I am not expecting you to start to memorize an entire page of a book at this point, that may come later if you are still interested in trying. For now, perhaps we can start with a much smaller and simpler exercise. The following list of vocabulary words is roughly **40 different vocabulary words**. What I want for you to do is to <u>look at this list of words</u> (don't write anything down for now) and try to use one of your memory palaces in order to store the data correctly. I would like for you to try to remember at least <u>4 words for each location</u> in your palace; you will need at least ten large enough locations in your palace.

Here, you will be challenged to try <u>to link two words together</u> to make a short story, or setting a scene, in your left field of vision in your mind, while also trying to link the next two words together in another short story, in your right hand field of vision. You will have exactly <u>5 minutes</u> to complete the exercise. Before you start, go over your memory palace and try to count each location and make sure you know which one is first, second, third, etc. As always, when you are done, go over your answers and give yourself <u>2.5 points</u> for each word correct. If you misspelled or put a word in the wrong order, then <u>no points</u> are awarded. Count up your total, this is your final score. Good luck, and here is the other list.

VOCABULARLY WORDS

1	race car
2	hamburgers
3	casket
4	marbles
5	tent
6	cigarettes
7	Yankee Stadium
8	poison ivy
9	gold
10	spacecraft
11	spiders
12	chocolate cake
13	fireworks

14	rainclouds
15	beer stein
16	earmuff
17	MP3 player
18	books
19	sail boat
20	stuffed animals
21	sand
22	coffee cup
23	envelopes
24	speaker phones
25	bills
26	alarm clock
27	door
28	throw rug
29	telephone
30	shredder
31	recliner chair
32	windows
33	stapler
34	CD rack
35	Holy Bible
36	surge outlet
37	lamp
38	lighthouse
39	radiator
40	mouse

Total score=

Total time=

Okay, I hope that I can still get the last word in before you get too tired (haha, another funny joke). Anyway, how did you do on his exercise? I know that it is not as easy as your think when it comes to picturing words. I continued to choose nouns for you, as they are much easier to delineate in your mind. The best thing to do if you get stuck on a certain word, is still to think of something that the word is similar to, or as we call it in the memory world, **the substitution word method**. You will hear a lot more about this concept in later chapters that deal with names and faces. But for now, let's say for instance that you don't know what Yankee Stadium (#7) looks like (I have been to both the old and the new one).

Well, all that you would have to do is try to think of something that is related to Yankee stadium, such as Lou Gehrig's retirement speech or the back picture silhouette of Babe Ruth with a baseball bat. Or you could use any other image that you can initially think of that reminds you of the words themselves. That way, there is really no word in the English vocabulary that you cannot visualize in one way or another. I will be giving you several different examples of how this can work with vocabulary words in the next chapters.

Here is another piece of advice I can give you in regards to memorizing long words, especially words with three or more syllables. One of the greatest things I learned about the English vocabulary is that certain words will usually begin with certain letters or phrases that are synonymous with other vocabulary words as well. Certain prefixes such as "acro", "inter", and "micro", can be thought of as actual images in of themselves. When I hear the prefix <u>acro</u>, I think of an acrobat, when I hear the prefix <u>inter</u>, I think of an entrance way sign, and when I think of the prefix <u>micro</u>, an image of a microscope comes to mind. This is good information to know when you are dealing with a rather long vocabulary word, as it is easier to break it up into different chunks. And one of the best ways to do so is to start with the beginning prefix. Here is a list of most of the <u>major prefixes</u> that are used in the English vocabulary today. See if you would like to create individual images for each and every word listed below, and then use that as a reference guide next time you see an extra-long vocabulary word that would make the average graduate college level student freak out.

Prefixes:

Acro, allo, alter, ante, anti, auto, bi, contra, counter, dis, down, dys, epi, extra, fore, hemi, hexa, hyper, hypo, ig, infra, inter, intra, macro, micro, mal, maxi, meso, meta, mid, mini, mis, mono, multi, non, octo, over, pan, para, penta, per, peri, poly, post, pre, pro, proto, pseudo, quadri, quasi, semi, sub, super, supra, tetra, trans, tri, ultra, un, under, up, xeno.

While most of us would probably find it difficult or have some uncertainties about how to create an image for a prefix of a word, there is another method that is quite literally something that we all grew up with when we were children. Most of us are familiar with the expression "abbreviations", which means to shorten the actual length of a piece of information in order to make it simpler to understand. For this instance, instead of using the word "abbreviations", we are going to use the phrase **"peg" or peg words.**

For example, when you see the peg letters "USA", we all know that this means, United States of America. When I think about this, I automatically think of a flag hovering over the continent of North America. Many of us would never question or second guess ourselves when it comes to coming up with an image that would suit the letters USA. However, it has become such an integral part of our vernacular today that we don't really even seem to think about it too much. Next time you see a long word, if you cannot seem to break it down into parts, you could also try to come up with some "peg word" or peg letters to simplify it, in order to make it both easier to remember and also easier to picture. Try this exercise for example, see if you can shorten or come up with only 3 or 4 letters to stand for or remind you of each the following words:

PEG WORD LIST:

Meticulous= possible MTU
Obsequious=possible OBQ
Personification=possible PSF

Vicarious=possible VCR
Sublimation= possible SBM

Also, even though we are focusing most of our vocabulary word memory skills on the English language, it does not mean that you cannot apply the same principles to <u>foreign vocabulary words</u> as well. I used to study Spanish while in high school, and I used to hate having to try to remember what the words meant and how to spell and say them. Now, by using the **substitution method**, you can make remembering foreign vocabulary words so much easier. All you have to do is decide what the word actually sounds like or looks like. For example, in Spanish, the word for school is "<u>escuela</u>", which sounds like the words "<u>ask</u>" and "<u>quail</u>". So, I could try to picture someone "asking" a "quail" where to find a school, and the quail is pointing at a building behind him that looks like a school, with a big letter "A" on it. Also, the Spanish word for heart is "<u>corazon</u>", which sounds like the words "core" and "zone". In this instance, I could picture an apple core lying inside of a construction zone area, where there is a human heart on a billboard above it. This works very well with nouns and action verbs, as well as many pronouns.

All you have to remember for foreign vocabulary words is to know what the <u>actual translation</u> of the word is, and then make up <u>a small story</u> about the word itself based on how it looks and sounds. Sometimes the word itself looks like something that you already know, so the comparison can be easy. And don't worry about having to figure out how to pronounce all the words all by yourself; most translation dictionaries provide you with information about how to say the words correctly, with the right pronunciations. Simply just repeat the word a few times to yourself to see what the word sounds like or reminds you of. And with that, you may one day be able to learn an entire foreign language on your own using this particular memory style, as well as the other vocabulary word memory methods that were previously taught.

And now for one last final word test, I would like for you to practice the same exercise that you did earlier with your numbers memory. In this instance, I am going to split up the larger list of words into two equal halves. That means that for now, you should have a total of three major lists of vocabulary words. I will be asking you to practice memorizing each list, one at a time, on a different day of the week, and to use a different memory palace for each exercise. You can use either the link method or the substitution method in any of your memory palaces. You will use the same physical materials that you used for the numbers memory challenges, such as papers and stopwatches, and will score yourself in the same way. Use one sheet of paper in order to write your answers as well as another one to cover up your materials if needed.

I have included the lists of words for your convenience, as well as a list for inputting your scores over the course of a week. Watch to see how much faster you get with each passing attempt. Do not do the same list more than one in a row before the next one; give your brain enough time to forget the words after a few days before you go back to trying it again. Notice how much improvement there is in your scores, and try to learn to really use your inner senses to create lasting images for each word. You will have 5 minutes for each exercise to remember the information, and then another 5 minutes for recall. If you feel like practicing with the same lists for another week, feel free and go ahead. Here are the lists of words in a whole new order for you. Good luck and have fun.

COLUMN 1	COLUMN 2	COLUMN 3
pillows	race car	Sand
calendar	hamburgers	coffee cup
office	casket	envelopes
flag	marbles	speaker phones
building	tent	Bills
barbecue	cigarettes	alarm clock
tombstones	Yankee Stadium	Door
Christmas tree	poison ivy	throw rug
soldier	gold	telephone
school	spacecraft	shredder
car	spiders	recliner chair
dog	chocolate cake	windows
computer	fireworks	stapler
library	rainclouds	CD rack
baseball bat	beer stein	Holy Bible
stove	earmuffs	surge outlet
airplane	MP3 player	Lamp
lightning	books	lighthouse
fireworks	sailboat	radiator
camel	stuffed animals	mouse
beer		
TV set		
ghosts		
basketball		
hole		
golf clubs		
robot		
chicken		
bathtub		
giraffe		

Here is a chart so that you can measure your progress throughout the week on this exercise.

DAY EXERCISE	SCORE (PERCENT/ CORRECT)	TIME (MINUTES, SECOND)
FIRST DAY		
SECOND DAY		
THIRD DAY		
FOURTH DAY		
FIFTH DAY		
SIXTH DAY		
SEVENTH DAY		

AVERAGE SCORE=

AVERAGE TIME=

CHAPTER 7

Binary codes and number memory

For those of you who thought that you were finally done with numbers memory tasks, looks like you are in for a disappointment. Not all numbers have to be complicated or overwhelming when it comes to memorizing them. Sometimes, even the most simple and straightforward combinations of numbers can seem overwhelming to most of us, especially when they are presented to us in an illogical sequences. When I was a child, I used to love watching boxing movies, particularly movies made during the 1980's. My all-time favorite boxing movie as a child (this should come as no surprise) was the hit movie, "**Rocky**", and all of its other related sequels. When I look back and watch Rocky punching back furiously against Apollo Creed during those amazing bouts, I sometimes begin to wonder about not only how many punches does Rocky actually throw at Apollo, but also how often does the "southpaw from Philadelphia" end up using his right hand instead of his left hand during the matches.

Think about the fact that even though you only have two hands to use, if you were asked to memorize the exact order of each and every punch that was thrown during a taped boxing match when shown in slow motion, you would probably have given up trying after just a few seconds due to the sheer amount of information (TKO to you, Rocky). However, if you could realize that boxers can only use either their left or their right hands to punch, then there is actually no other third option to use. And so for that matter, don't think of it as the boxer is throwing a <u>right hand punch,</u> think of it as he is <u>NOT throwing a left hand punch</u>. Does this seem to make more sense when I phrase it like that? If so, then get ready for a whole new memory challenge ahead of you that deals with similar numerical presentations. This next chapter deals with a concept that is often used for basic memory tasks such as this, and can be better summed up in just two words to describe it: **binary codes**.

When I was growing up and going to high school during the 1990's, the internet itself had barely come into existence. We were still using the Dewey Decimal system in order to locate our library books during certain classes. Now of days, all you have to do is just click a few buttons on a computer, and you can know more information about just one book than having to spend an hour using the Dewey Decimal system. When I was a junior in high school, we had one of our first ever computer technology classes offered to us, where I was first introduced to things like an Apple computer, Microsoft Power Point, and spreadsheets. (those were the good old days). However, during that course, the teacher never truly got into explaining what binary codes really were, and what they had to do with anything computer related. It was not until 3 years later in 1999, did a major motion picture, regarding humans and AI computer androids, finally shed some light on this otherwise unfamiliar subject matter known as **binary coding.**

If you have ever seen the science fiction action movie "The Matrix", you are aware of the title character played called Neo (that is the word ONE spelled differently, another memory tickler). Anyway, his arch enemy is a fictitious super-powered special agent conveniently named Smith. At the end of the movie, the only way for Neo to defeat his technologically advanced adversary, is to be able to see him as well as his surrounding counterpart colleagues, through visualized computer programming codes, known as <u>binary codes</u>. In this scene, Neo is able to visualize everything around him in terms of random sets of binary coding.

If you have never seen a binary code before, it is simply just a long strand of the numbers 0 and 1 mixed together. An example might look like this; **100011110001001100011001001000**. This seems almost impossible to memorize when you look at it, as there is always a 50%

chance of getting the numbers wrong (remember, there are only 0's and 1's, similar to lefts and rights). However, going back to the original discussion about the Dominic System, there is a way to chunk this information into separate parts, and make the numbers look a lot more interesting to memorize. I will show you the same information again, only this time it will look like this: **100/011/110/001/001/100/0 11/001/001/ 000**. Now, what do you think about the number?

One technique that the great Dominic O'Brien came up with for such memorization purposes, was the ability to take sequences of three numbers at a time, and then change those sequences into one singular digit. For example, when he put together the number **001**, he reminded himself that it looked like just the <u>number 1</u> itself. So, for this particular style of memorization, the number **001** would translate to <u>01, or the letters OA</u> (remember from your previous 100 character images from before, same principle). The number **000** would translate to <u>00</u> or just the letters OO, and so on. For a full list of all of the possible binary code combinations and their corresponding letters and numbers, here is a reference chart that Dominic created to help you make more sense of this.

$$
\begin{aligned}
&\textbf{000} = \textbf{(0) OO}\\
&\textbf{001} = \textbf{(1) OA}\\
&\textbf{011} = \textbf{(2) OB}\\
&\textbf{111} = \textbf{(3) OC}\\
&\textbf{110} = \textbf{(4) OD}\\
&\textbf{100} = \textbf{(5) OE}\\
&\textbf{010} = \textbf{(6) OS}\\
&\textbf{101} = \textbf{(7) OG}
\end{aligned}
$$

So, for the previously <u>mentioned binary number,</u> you could visualize it as the following:

100/011/110/001/001/100/011/001/001/000= (5 / 2 / 4 / 1 / 1 / 5 / 2 / 1 / 1 / 0)

(that is literally **52 41 15 21 10**)

For those of us out there wondering just how to make sense of such an illogical looking chart, here is another way to interpret the numbers as you see them. As you probably already know, the first four numbers (**000, 001, 011, 111**) seem pretty self-explanatory. You just simply <u>count</u> the number of 1's and then add up the total. (011=2, 111=3) However, when you get to the other numbers (**110, 100, 010, 101**), things get a little bit more complicated at this point. Another way to try to make it easier for yourself is to make up stories for some of the numbers that remind you of actual letters. For me, the number **101** look like a <u>goal post with a football</u> going through it, therefore I am able to remember the letter <u>G</u> for goal post. The number **100** reminds me of a <u>dollar bill</u> (100 cents), or simply the word <u>MONEY</u>. Money only has five letters in it, therefore 100 resembles the number 5 or OE.

By remembering what character images or persons you created for the numbers **00-07**, you should already know what images in your head you can imagine for each set of binary codes. And the best thing is that, you can remember <u>three different numbers</u> in a binary code for just <u>one single letter</u> of your memory alphabet. This should help out a lot with most of the combinations of binary numbers, the rest I leave up to you go decipher. And if you have your own way of remembering the combinations of numbers and codes as described, go right ahead and use that for yourself.

I am sure that many of us at home are wondering when you will ever have to memorize binary codes in your life. It could be if you are either a computer geek or someone just trying to save Zion from the immortal powers of the Agents of Change (watch the movies if you don't get the euphemism). The point is that you don't have to simply memorize binary codes in order to use this particular memory system. The only thing that you can really use this system for, is to memorize materials that only have <u>two random quantities</u> or variables to present, such as rights and lefts, ups and down, or black and whites. One favorite activity that I like to do for people is to memorize the order of the colors of a deck of cards. (we will get into how to memorize the actual cards in the next coming chapter, for now this is just a warm up).

For anybody that has ever seen a deck of cards, the only two colors located in the deck, are red and black. Therefore, when you see a red card, what you are actually seeing is either a red card or just a card that is not black (as in the left and right punch theory stated earlier). If you want to memorize the actual order of the colors, all you have to do is decide which color will be your primary color, so that you don't have to actually remember every single card itself. Just realize, all the diamonds and hearts are **red**, all the spades and clubs are **black**. So, if I were try to memorize the card colors of a card deck according to the binary code principle, I would take three cards at a time and look at the first, second and third cards. The reds can stand for either 0 or 1, and the blacks could also stand for either 0 or 1, whichever card you want to be your primary.

For me, I chose to make red equal to **1** and black equal to **0**. So, if the first card in a three card pile is red, and the next is black and the final is black, then it would look like 100, or 05 or E. If the next pile of three cards has the first card as black, the second card as red and the third card as red, then it would like look 011 or OB or 2. Therefore, the previous six cards could be translated into the letters EB (or the **E**aster **B**unny), or 100 011. (these are the first six numbers of the previous binary code number that I gave you) Try this out sometime with a deck of cards, use only three cards at a time and make sure you know which color you want as your primary, and which one is the secondary. Then just translate the order of the colors according to the previous binary codes list stated. This can help you to become more familiar with binary codes in general, if you wish to study such a subject.

However, if you would like to know another way to memorize a deck of cards in terms of the order of colors, there is a different method that does not have anything to do with the Dominic System of binary codes. In fact, I found out this method one day while eating lunch at a diner. One day, while I was sitting in a diner eating a Panini sandwich, I could not help but notice that the upper **t**op piece of bread was **t**oasted, the **m**iddle was stuffed with **m**eat, and the **b**ottom was **b**urnt due to being in the machine too long. All of a sudden, I just realized, while I was cleaning my cloth off with my napkins, that I had stumbled upon a mnemonic that could very well change the way I memorized binary codes that were grouped in pairs. At that moment, I realized that there was another way to make sense of binary code information; however it was not as complete and organized as the previous method was.

In this instance, I was connecting letters to describe different parts of the sandwich. You only need 3 cards for each letter, and one card is on top, another is in the middle, and the third is on the bottom. Remember that the **t**op of the sandwich was **t**oasted (letter T), the **mi**ddle had **m**eat in it (letter M) and the **b**ottom was **b**urnt (letter B). After that, I also realized that if all 3 of the cards in this imaginary situation were the same primary color, than I could substitute the letter A to stand for **A**LL. And if none of the cards were the primary color I had picked, than I could substitute the letter **O** for **0** or zer**o**.

Therefore, the letters that I came up with for such memory purposes were **A, O, T, M, B**. If my primary color (either red or black) was on top of the first group of three cards, then that letter would be T. If my primary color was at the bottom of the three cards, then that letter would be letter B. And if my primary color was in the middle, then that letter would be M, and so on and so forth. Unfortunately, this does not help you when you primary color comes up only twice, such as top/middle or middle/bottom. For that combo you would have to make up something like **TM** for top and middle, and **MB** for middle and bottom. If you are familiar with anagrams, the only letters that you really have to work with are **A, O, T, M, B, TM, MB**. So, try to think of your own words or come up with actual words from this combination of letters, and use that for a cool memory stunt in the future. If you really interested in challenging yourself, then look at the following list of cards below. Make sure that you perhaps substitute red for your primary color. Then, while going from left to right in order, I dare you to spell out the following combination of cards and see how easy the final imagery will be:

red/red/red   red/black/black
black/black/black   black/red/black   black/black/red
black/black/black   black/red/black   black/black/red.
(Hint, think of Hiroshima World War II)

In addition, I would like to present one last challenge for binary code memorization. Below I have listed out 60 different digits of binary code for you to memorize. You will be quizzed on this, so take out a piece of paper and a stopwatch for this exercise, just like you have done before. First, write out the exact order of the numbers on one sheet of paper big enough so that you can read it. Then get out your stopwatch and prepare to time yourself. In this instance, I would like for you to have 5 minutes to memorize the information, and then 5 minutes for recall on another sheet of paper.

Once you are done with the memorization part, turn over your initial sheet of paper and write out the number sequence on the other sheet of paper. Remember, try to visualize each set of three numbers as just one letter or number, and then try to combine at least two or three sets of binary codes together to equal just one giant image. And then place those images in your memory palace. Then do the same for the next set of two or three groupings of binary codes. Give yourself 1 point for each group of three binary codes you memorize correctly, with a maximum score of 20. Get ready, get set, and go for it.

010 011 001 110 100 000 100 100 001 000 111 110 010 011 111 001 110 100 000 011

TOTAL TIME:

TOTAL SCORE:

CHAPTER 8

(card memorization) The Dominic Method again

Back when my late maternal grandfather was still alive, he used to teach me various card games as a way to pass the time. Games such as Gin Rummy, 5 card poker, War, and Solitaire were just a few of the games that he himself had learned as a child growing up in Italy. There were countless days, sitting there in Grandma's old Italian style kitchen area, where we would sit down and play hand after hand of these old school card games together. Yet I remember that, even though it looked as though he was not always paying attention to his hands, he always seemed to know actually what cards he needed in order to win.

And despite my best efforts to play, he usually did win each hand. At first I thought that my grandfather was either some kind of card shark or perhaps just lucky enough to win a card game against his 8 year old grandson. However, it was not until I read my first memory book almost thirty years later, did I realize that there was an actual method and science that my grandfather was probably using, which explains the art of **card memorization**.

So, I bet all of you are starting to get tired of all of these randomly different areas of information to memorize. I suppose you are just hoping to finally relax and have a little fun for once. Well, I can't say that I blame you for wanting to just kick back a little. I think that it is time to find something that will make you feel some sense of enjoyment and thrill. When I first got started in the whole memory sports business, I was initially interested in learning how to memorize playing cards. Although I was not a professional gambler at the time (I have gotten kicked out of a few poker games with some friends unfortunately), I just wanted to be able to learn how to recall a certain number of cards from the deck, and then try to impress my friends and loved ones by reciting them back through memory. Needless to say, this was going to become my first real opportunity to broadcast my talents to those around me who thought that what I about to do was really impossible.

This is also the same idealistic feeling that the great Dominic O Brien first felt when he was first inspired to get involved in the field of memory sports. During the late 1980's, Dominic was watching a TV show on BBC television where he saw a magician and memory performer with the initials **C.C** get up on stage and perform in front of a live studio audience. During this magician's performance, the entertainer told the crowd that he was going to memorize all 52 playing cards in a deck in less than 5 minutes with perfect recall. He was going to shuffle the deck a few times and then remember the order of the cards both forwards, backwards, and the exact location of every single individual card.

The host and the audience thought that this was a joke or that the deck was probably rigged. However, he later produced a deck of cards and had the deck shuffled several times by someone else to prove that this was not a hoax. He then looked at each individual card and ran through the deck, one card at a time, until he was all finished after just 3 minutes of memorization! He then put the deck away, closed his eyes and then recited the exact order of the entire deck of cards from start to finish without making a single mistake! Dominic was in shock, and the audience did not know what to think of this. The audience had just witnessed a man look at an entire deck of 52 playing cards, and produce complete photographic memory of its contents in less than 200 seconds. It was this moment that propelled Dominic to embark upon his own memory journey into the field of mnemonics.

When I first heard this story, I thought that it was too good to be true. How could a person look at each card in a deck, observe the picture and graphics associated with each card, and then be able to come up with an image in their head to help them remember it later on? I initially felt that there must be some shortcut or some trick to explain how something so astronomical could ever be done. Or perhaps the host had missed something, and that C.C had somehow not really shuffled the deck as the cards might have been fixed.

But later on, when I read through Dominic's books and learned about his memory techniques, I realized that the methods for memorizing cards were strangely similar to the methods that he had used in remembering numbers. He simply had figured out a way to convert numbers to equal card symbols, and then had used the same rubric to remember the actual name and suit of such card. (think it is impossible, well don't bet on it)

Previously, I believe you remember me lecturing you about the mnemonic system for numbers and how to convert a two digit number into two letters. And then to convert those two letters into an image of a person, character, action or object. Well, guess what? The same thing can be done for playing cards; you just have to know how to decode the cards into something that is memorable. For example, if I look at the 4 of Clubs, I instantly think of the number 43, which translates into the letter DC, or Dick Clark from the NYC New Year's Eve festival. Now, you might be wondering how I came up with the numbers 43 from the 4 of Clubs? Well, the way it works is this: you first take the actual <u>number</u> of the card (Ace =1, 2=2, 3=3, etc) and just make that the first number in your sequence. In this case, the 4 in the 4 of Clubs would be the letter D. Next, you think of the <u>first LETTER</u> of the <u>suit</u> of the cards. In this case, the suit of the card is the Clubs, and Clubs starts with the letter C. And C equals 3 according to the Dominic system of memory. Hence, I would come up with the numbers 43 to represent the 4 of Clubs, or the letters DC.

It is so fortunate to realize that the first letter of such of the 4 suits in a card deck can be found in the alphabet codes of the **Dominic System**. Remember earlier that A=1, B=2, C=3 and so on. Well, Aces would equal 1 as the word Ace starts with the letter <u>A.</u> Spades starts with the letter <u>S</u> and S equals the number 6 in the code. Diamonds start the letter <u>D</u> and D relates to the number 4. And Hearts starts with the letter <u>H</u> and H relates to the number 8. For those of you that need a reminder of the Dominic System letter/number coding system, here it is again.

Number	1	2	3	4	5	6	7	8	9	0
Mnemonic	A	B	C	D	E	S	G	H	N	O

This should make it easier for you when it comes to memorizing cards because you probably already have 100 different character images or persons created for your number memory system. This means that you already have an image for at <u>least 40 of the 52 cards</u> in your deck already memorized. Just in case you are confused, you can always substitute the number 10 in a deck of cards to equal the letter O, as I do not want you using the letter J for this number, which is the tenth letter of the alphabet. Therefore, the 10 of Spades would be OS, as 10 is the number and S is for Spades. The only problem with this system is that it does not help you to remember any of the 12 face cards such <u>as Jacks, Queens and Kings</u>.

Unfortunately, that is something you will have to work on in your own way. As far as how I myself have gone about doing this, I have used the initials of each face card to come up with <u>an additional 12 new characters</u> or images of my own (yes, looks like your company of <u>100 images</u> has just grown to 112 for now). And by the way, the reason why I didn't want you to use the letter J for the number 10 is because the letter J can be confused with the word <u>Jack</u> in a deck of cards. Here is a list for how to come up with codes or images for the remaining twelve face cards in a deck.

Jack of Clubs= JC	Queen of Clubs= QC	King of Clubs= KC
Jack of Spades= JS	Queen of Spades= QS	King of Spades= KS
Jack of Diamonds= JD	Queen of Diamonds= QD	King of Diamonds= KD
Jack of Hearts= JH	Queen of Hearts= QH	King of Hearts= KH

Just in case you needed any further help with determining what your <u>mental images</u> are for your <u>individual playing cards</u>, I have enclosed another chart for your references:

Ace of Clubs	AC	13
2 of Clubs	BC	23
3 of Clubs	CC	33
4 of Clubs	DC	43
5 of Clubs	EC	53
6 of Clubs	SC	63
7 of Clubs	GC	73
8 of Clubs	HC	83
9 of Clubs	NC	93
10 of Clubs	OC	03
Ace of Spades	AS	16
2 of Spades	BS	26
3 of Spades	CS	36
4 of Spades	DS	46
5 of Spades	ES	56
6 of Spades	SS	66
7 of Spades	GS	76
8 of Spades	HS	86
9 of Spades	NS	96
10 of Spades	OS	06
Ace of Diamonds	AD	14
2 of Diamonds	BD	24
3 of Diamonds	CD	34
4 of Diamonds	DD	44
5 of Diamonds	ED	54
6 of Diamonds	SD	64
7 of Diamonds	GD	74
8 of Diamonds	HD	84
9 of Diamonds	ND	94

10 of Diamonds	OD	04
Ace of Hearts	AH	18
2 of Hearts	BH	28
3 of Hearts	CH	38
4 of Hearts	DH	48
5 of Hearts	EH	58
6 of Hearts	SH	68
7 of Hearts	GH	78
8 of Hearts	HH	88
9 of Hearts	NH	98
10 of Hearts	OH	08

As for now, it would be a good idea to go over every one of the 52 characters or persons you have previously assigned for each of your numbered cards and your face cards. Try not to get distracted by the images of the cards itself; most memory athletes tend to make the mistake of actually looking at the card itself and then eventually looking at the top left hand corner. You will have to train your brain to avoid looking at the card itself and instead only focus on the top left hand corner of each card and look at the related symbols. In any standard deck of cards, the number of card will appear higher on the top, and then the symbol of the suit will appear directly underneath it.

Try to spend some time getting used to the actual symbols for each suit, as this is an area that tends to confuse many memory athletes, as we have an easier time noticing the numbers or letters of a card rather than the suit symbols. In case you would like to have an easier way to remember the actual symbol codes for each suit of a card deck, we already know what hearts and diamonds look like, and they are both red for every deck. The symbol for clubs has a shape that has 3 cloves on it, therefore the word Clubs starts with C, and C stands for 3. This should make it easier to identity the remaining suit.

If can you remember the previous lesson about setting the scene with memory images, let's try to memorize 4 random cards, such as the

2 of Spades, the 4 of Clubs, the 6 of Hearts, and the 8 of Diamonds. Use your memory palace technique by placing two cards at each location, one of the left side and one on the right side. So, I if I wanted to remember the first card, which is the 2 of Spades, I would think of the letters BS or the number 26, as the 2 itself would represent the letter B, and Spades starts with the letter S, which can be substituted for the number 6. For this, I picture Bart Simpson (BS), throwing confetti in the air (DC) as Dick Clark would do on New Year's Day. Standing next to him, I would imagine the letters SH or the number 68, as the 6 itself would represent the letter S, and Hearts starts with the letter H, which can be substituted for the number 8.

For this, I picture Sherlock Holmes (68) looking through a magnifying glass. Standing to the right of him, I would imagine the letters HD or the number 84, as the 8 itself would represent the letter H, and Diamonds starts with the letter D, which can be substituted for the number 4. For this, I picture a High Def television set (84). So, in this particular series of cards, I am picturing Bart Simpson throwing confetti in the air, while on his right side stands Sherlock Holmes, looking through a magnifying glass at a large TV set that is broken. And there you have it; all four cards are perfectly memorized.

I think you remember from earlier at the beginning of the book, that I gave you an initial test of your ability to recall the exact order of over half a deck of cards (30) from your very first exercise. You were allowed 5 minutes to look over the list, then cover it up and write out the answers using your old method of memorization. Well, now you have already learned a whole new method of memory improvement for cards. It is time to see if you can improve upon your past performance. (hope you still have the originals scores from the beginning) You will be doing the same memory test again, looking at the answers for _five_ minutes, then covering up the page, and giving yourself _5 minutes_ for recall. You don't have to write out the exact original information if you don't want to, you can use abbreviations if it helps make it easier. See how well you have improved since your first attempt. In case you don't have it with you, here it is again. Good luck.

Ace of Spades
2 of Hearts
10 of Clubs
4 of Diamonds
6 of Clubs
Jack of Diamonds
Queen of Spades
Ace of Hearts
2 of Clubs
9 of Hearts
8 of Clubs
10 of Spades
6 of Diamonds
7 of Clubs
8 of Diamonds
Jack of Hearts
King of Diamonds
King of Clubs
Queen of Hearts
Jack of Spades
4 of Clubs
2 of Spades
9 of Spades
9 of Diamonds
5 of Spades
5 of Clubs
Queen of Clubs
8 of Spades
2 of Diamonds
7 of Diamonds

Okay, I think it would only be fair of me to expect you to be able to remember the <u>remaining cards</u> that have not been called yet from the deck. Don't worry, there are <u>only 22 left</u>, as I already had you memorize 30 from before (there are only 52 cards in a deck). So, this one should be easier than the other one. Since this section of the deck is shorter than the first one, instead of giving you 5 minutes to memorize it, I will be giving you only <u>4 minutes</u> to memorize it and <u>5 minutes</u> of recall again. Follow the same procedures as before with regards to covering up the answers and writing your responses on another sheet of paper. You don't have to write out the exact original information if you don't want to. The following cards to recall for your <u>second attempt</u> at card memory are the following: Good luck.

3 of Diamonds
7 of Spades
10 of Hearts
5 of Hearts
9 of Clubs
3 of Clubs
6 of Spades
4 of Spades
Queen of Diamonds
Ace of Clubs
4 of Hearts
5 of Diamonds
Ace of Diamonds
6 of Hearts
3 of Spades
8 of Hearts
King of Spades
7 of Hearts
King of Hearts
10 of Diamonds
3 of Hearts
Jack of Clubs

Well, at this point, I think that instead of giving you another assignment to work on, perhaps now it would be a good idea to give you a break and let you go and find a deck of playing cards for yourself. Please remove the joker cards and any other non-playing cards from such deck. When you have a chance, locate the deck of cards, get out a stopwatch, shuffle the deck once or twice, and try to time yourself to see how fast you can memorize the <u>whole 52 card deck</u> on your own. I will not tell you how much time you are required to have, as I don't want to put too much pressure on you (lord knows, I have probably done so already). For now, just practice at least a few times during the week, usually once a day for now, and then record your scores on the table below. Make sure you mix the deck and shuffle it accordingly after each memory round (usually 3-4 shuffles). Remember, if you get a card wrong, just <u>count up</u> however many cards you got right before that mistake, this will give you your <u>base score</u>. Try this out at least once a day for a week and see how well you do. Perhaps one day, even you will be able to outwit and outsmart most of the card sharks in Vegas. Good luck and get ready to go all in.

DAY EXERCISE	SCORE (CORRECT) of 52	TIME (MINUTES, SECOND)
FIRST DAY		
SECOND DAY		
THIRD DAY		
FOURTH DAY		
FIFTH DAY		
SIXTH DAY		
SEVENTH DAY		

AVERAGE SCORE=

AVERAGE TIME=

CHAPTER 9

Names and faces (Hello, have we met before?)

A lot of times, I find myself unable to recall a person's name, but for some reason, their face looks very familiar. Does this seem like something we have all been through at one time or another? Trust me, there is nothing wrong with you if you have forgotten a person's name but can still remember their face. We are creatures of <u>visual recall</u>, which means that we tend to pay more attention to <u>what we see</u> than to <u>what we hear</u>. So, unless of course every person you ever meet just happens to walk around with a large name tag around their necks, then chances are that you will have to eventually rely upon your auditory memory to recall people's names as opposed to your visual memory.

This explains one of the most common apologizes ever heard by human beings, which is "I am so sorry, I remember your face, but I don't remember your name". However, before you start to think that this type of interpersonal social error is bound to happen to you all the time, let me talk to you a little bit about how to improve your **ability to recall <u>names and faces</u>,** so that next time you meet someone new in your life, you are not "faced" with this same uncomfortable and slightly offensive situation again.

When my late paternal grandfather was alive back in the 1940's, there was a time when he was able to serve in the Marine Corps while being stationed over in Japan. During that time, the current president of the United States was a man from my home state of New York, famously known as Franklin Delano Roosevelt. At that time, very few of us even knew that this great and powerful man, whom the country looked up to for so many reasons, was secretly unable to even stand up or walk on his own two legs. Yet, most rhetorical historians would agree that, when it comes to the idea of the presidency, image itself is more important than actions.

That being said, a lot of people who were alive during that time have mentioned that, if they had been able to own a television set in their households and had watched FDR during his numerous speeches, it would have been unlikely that this country, which was already recovering from a Great Depression and World War II, would have ever chosen to elect a man who was sitting in a wheelchair all day. However, there was one individual behind the scenes who was working on FDR's inner staff. And this one person seemed to know a lot more about how to influence the general public as far as of making the voters see past FDR's physical handicaps, and instead focusing their attention more on his political character.

That gentleman's name was **James Farley**, and he was a legend among the political kingpins of his time, and was probably one of the greatest politician campaign managers of the twentieth century. However, in the memory world, he was also a legend for being able to recall the names and faces of a lot of the most powerful and rich benefactors that FDR had ever met in the course of his presidency. And he did this by creating something that is still widely used to this day, called a Farley file. In such a file, he would include a photograph of the face of the person that FDR had met, as well as some personal data written down about each individual that he could commit to memory (I will tell you later how to remember personal data in a future chapter).

And by remembering the names and personal data of all of the most important people that FDR was counting on to get re-elected on his campaign trail, this small town, farm working high school dropout, was able to get FDR the political money and the electoral votes needed to help him get re-elected more than once (that was a point of contention that existed between the two of them, but I will let you look that information up at a later date). It just goes to show you that remembering a person's name can go a long way when you want to get support from others.

In addition, there was another small town, farm working high school dropout, who also understood the importance of remembering names and faces around the same time in US history. He is probably one of the famous self-help and motivational speakers of the past century, and his name was **Dale Carnegie**. In his influential book, "How to Win Friends and Influence People", he dedicated one chapter of his book to the importance of being able to recall people's names when talking to them, as well as the associated feelings that these people have after being recognized for such an act.

He also explains why it is so important to remember personal data about a person as well as their name, and to use all of this information in order to influence people to your way of thinking. He always said that a person's name was the "most special and sensitive possession" that a person could have in the course of their lifetime. Think about it, even after we are dead and all of our worldly possessions are gone, and our personal legacy is all but forgotten from the history books, our names will still be sketched into our tombstones for decades to come. Wouldn't it be better to remember a person's name now while they are still alive as opposed to remembering it only when they are already dead?

That being said, now would be a good time to go over some of the fundamentals on how best to remember people's names and faces as well as some of the techniques that are used both by memory athletes and everyday average people. First of all, nobody in this world walks around with a name tag around their neck everyday to make it easier for us to recall their names. (less you are working in a prison like I used to) If that were the case, this chapter would not be necessary and most of us would just have to read people's name tags as opposed to using our brains.

However, before I go on to show you some strategies that you can use in either your competitive life or personal life, let me introduce you to yet another famous memory expert who has revolutionized the topic of name and facial recall. He is the world's foremost expert on memory training, who, although retired and living in a nursing home, has spent over 55 years of his life teaching people across the county about his methods of memory enhancement and memorization, particularly first and last name recall. He is commonly referred in the memory world as "Yoda" (again, another Star Wars reference to an old and learned Jedi grand master), and his initials are H.L.

Back in 1988, I remember sitting down and watching an episode of the Tonight Show with Johnny Carson. During that episode, there were several guests being interviewed, including this 62 year old magician from NYC named **H.L**. On the episode, as well as all other segments during its series, there was a live studio audience that was actually watching the Tonight show from the auditorium seats. H.L, during the beginning and intermission segments of the show, had gotten up and walked around the room and through the audience quietly, asking each and every person about their last names without telling them what was going on. What people did not realize was that he was about to surprise them in few minutes in a way they could never have anticipated.

Towards the end of the show, Johnny Carson called H.L back on stage to promote his book on memory techniques, and to answer just a few questions about memory improvement. It was then that I saw this man do something that I thought was incredible. H.L. later got up out his chair, again went into the studio audience with a microphone, and then asked all of the spectators to stand up out of seats, and wait for him to be able to call out their names before they could be seated again. One by one, H.L. pointed at each individual person (there had to be at least 100 people), called out each person's last name to them, and eventually in just a few minutes, every single person who was standing had already sat down. He had literally remembered the names of over 100 people in less than one hour and had recalled exactly where they were sitting. This was completely unheard of at the time.(unless you remember the previous story of Simonides of Ceo) But before I get ahead of myself, let me show you how he did it and what methods you too can take to hopefully one day accomplish such a miraculous feat of name and face memory (even if you don't get on the Tonight Show anyway).

First and foremost, let's take a moment to review what exact components actually make up a human face (unless of course you have never seen an actual person before). Many of us take for granted what a human face really looks like, as we all have the same features on our heads. Eyes, ears, nose, mouth, teeth, jaw, neck, cheeks and eyebrows are just a few of the similarities that we all are born with. Hairlines, skin tone, piercings, baldness, and possible tattoos are other features that we can accumulate later in life, depending on our health and life style choices. And the best part is that while most of us normally exit our homes in the morning fully clothed and covered up, the one part of the body that always remains naked in our daily lives is our face. So, in order to better understand what makes a face really look like a face, let's try to examine and delineate the various parts of a human face.

Without getting into too much medical terminology, there are at <u>least 14 different areas</u> of the average human face that can be identified just at looking at them. They are the **hair, the forehead, the temple, the eyelashes, the eyebrows, the eyes, the ears, the cheeks, the nostrils, the nose, the earlobes, the lips, the jaw and the chin.** The hair is usually located on top of the head, it can be short or long, think or balding, combed or disheveled, and multiple different colors. The forehead can have lines, be short or long, and have multiple complexions on it. Eyebrows can be close or separate, thin or bushy, long or short, large or invisible. Eyes can be multiple different colors, close or far apart, and glasses can be worn. Ears can be pointed or flat, large or small, multiple earrings, and possibly concealed by the hair. Cheeks can be rosy or white, full or flat, colored or pale, and have multiple levels of make-up attached. Noses can be pointed or large, tall or small, red or pale, or have piercings or mustaches near them. And finally, jaws and chins can be strong or weak, round or squared, or covered with facial hair or other piercings. The list goes on and on about the different possible locations on a face that could actively get your attention and make you focus on that one area.

In order to better get yourself acquainted with the various contours and designs of a human face, one of the best ways to get started on learning how to look at a face, is to look at a digital or up-close photographic image of either yourself or someone else you know. This can be easily done on social media or by looking at a self-portrait of someone. If you have the chance to acquire such an object, please take a few minutes to look at it, observe each individual section of the face, and take note of what seems to strike you most as being odd or noticeable about the particular face. Believe me, nobody has a boring or manikin like face in this world. There is always something special or unique about each person's face. Try to spend some time looking at each section of the face; write out the list of features described earlier if this helps to remember all of the areas. Try to really notice each area and decide for yourself what makes each section of the face boring or not boring. This will help you to develop better observation abilities than just trying to stare at another human person's face endlessly while they look back at you in terror (my mother always said that it is not polite to stare too long).

Some of the simplest ways to remember a person's name and face can be done in our everyday interactions and conversations with people in our lives. There are **7 different steps** that can help you to recall people's names and faces better during real life interactions. These steps have been used and tested before, and have helped countless people become better able to recall names and faces.

First, look directly at the person while you talk to them, while also trying to minimize or ignore any other distractions or sounds around you. Do this for only a few seconds. Second, look for something about their face that you either admire or find to be interesting or unique (even identical twins such as I still have noticeable characteristics that distinguish the two of us). Third, ask the person what their name is and to tell it to you both slowly and clearly. Try to lean in or put your hand to your ear in order to better hear them. Fourth, repeat the name out loud to them in the course of a short introductory conversation by saying it least 3 times. You can follow this by thanking them for giving you their name in the first place. (don't' repeat their names 3 times in a row too fast as it might look robotic to the other person, simply use their name in at least 3 different sentences for an initial introduction).

Fifth, just in case the name does not sound simple or easy to you, ask the person if they can either spell it for you or if they use a nickname for themselves (this will help you to review the information more as you are trying to remember it). Sixth, try to either mention out loud or quietly to yourself if possible, whether or not the name reminds you of someone you already know personally or indirectly (family, friend, and celebrity). <u>Seventh and final</u>, while doing this, try to locate the point on the person's face that you found to be most intriguing, and then try to create an image in your mind that reminds you of the significance of the person's name. Also, just to be safe, when you are done talking with the person, spend a few seconds reviewing the information in your head afterwards, make sure you got it right, and then ask them if you got their name right by saying "Did you say that your name was ___"?

Now this seems not too difficult, as long as you are not surrounded by a large group of people at the same time and don't have to divide your attention to more than one person at once. In addition, if you are alone with such person for a few minutes, this also gives you the chance to get to know the person better, even if the conversation is brief and to the point. The one main thing that most people don't realize when it comes to memorizing names and faces is not that you really forgot what the person's name was when you met them. It is that you actually never even heard or paid attention to them saying their name in the first place.

By following these 7 steps (to help remember think about **lucky number 7** which works for a jackpot casino), you will be forcing yourself to <u>really hear, listen to,</u> and pay attention to what the person is telling you. This will help in being able to late recall their names even hours later during the day. Remember, this usually works best when you are trying to recall people's first names in casual conversations or semi-formal business meetings.

The first six steps seem elementary and self-explanatory to most people who are familiar with basic social etiquette at most major gatherings. However, the final step seems to be the one step that most people have never heard of or even tried before when it comes to memorizing names. The 7th stage is where you try to come up with various images of your own to represent each person's first and last name so that it is more meaningful to you. This is where you will have to look at the person's face and try to find something about it that is special, and then attach that imaginary image to it that point on the face.

This is important because there is a chance that you will come across a person in your life who has a first and last name that are so completely foreign to you, that you will have no frame of reference available later to recall it. And no matter how many times you try to rehearse the previous 6 steps in the list, without an idea of any images or characters that could be assigned to a person's name, there is little chance that you will be able to recall that person's name days or even hours later, unless you rehearse it multiple times. This is where we will dive back into an older subject matter that I briefly introduced to you during our discussion of memorizing vocabulary words. And that subject is called the **substitution method**.

One of the most basic things about trying to remember names for other people is to make the name meaningful or outrageous in your mind so that you don't forget it later on. In order to do this, it is necessary for you to come up with certain images or symbols in your mind to help you associate a person's name with such an image. The best way to get started in doing this is simply by making up a list of the most common first names you can think of for both men and women. There are so many different last names in this world, that I cannot devote an entire book towards them. If you ever get a chance to read The Memory Book by Harry Lorayne, he includes a list of over 500 last names with related images or symbols to help remember them.

However, since we don't have the time to go over all of the most common last names in the world right now, let's try to make up our own list for just first names for now. Be advised, this is just a rudimentary list of common first names for people here in the US, it does not include all the names that most people commonly use on a regular basis, so if I exclude or forget to include anybody's first name on this list, I deeply apologize. So, in order to use the substitution method for names, try to ask yourself **what the name actually looks or sounds like**.

Go over and think about each name one at a time, and think of the first thing that such name reminds you of (sounds, sights, personal relative). For instance, the name Abby sounds like a "bee", and the name Amy sounds like the command "to aim". So, if I was being introduced to a woman with the name Abby, I would try to locate a specific location on her face and then try to imagine bees swarming out of it. As well, if I met a woman named Amy, I would try to imagine a bull-eye target on a specific location of her face as well. It would be a good idea to create a written list for all of these names yourself, unless of course you think that you can remember the images without writing them down, it is your choice. Here are the lists for the most common female and male first names in the US.

COMMON FIRST NAMES FOR WOMEN:

Abby, Abigail, Adele, Alice, Allison, Amy, Angie, Angela, Ann, Anita, Annette, Annie, Annabelle, April, Audrey, Barbara, Beatrice, Becky, Belinda, Bernadette, Beth, Betty, Beverly, Billie, Bobbie, Bonnie, Brenda, Bridget, Britney, Camille, Cameron, Candy, Carla, Carmen, Carol, Celeste, Charlotte, Cheryl, Chloe, Chris, Chrissy, Christy, Christine, Cicely, Cindy, Claudia, Clare, Clara, Clarice, Connie, Crystal, Daphne, Darlene, Debbie, Deborah, Debra, Delia, Denise, Diana, Dina, Donna, Doris, Dorothy, Eileen, Elaine, Eleanor, Elise, Elizabeth, Ellen, Elle, Ellie, Emily, Erica, Eva, Evelyn, Faith, Felicia, Florence, Frances, Gabby, Gabriella, Gayle, Georgia, Gina, Ginny, Ginger, Glenda, Gloria, Grace, Gwen, Hannah, Harriet, Heather, Heidi, Helen, Holly, Hope, Iris, Irene, Isla, Ivy, Jackie, Jacqueline, Jamie, Jan, Jane, Janice, Jean, Jeanette, Jennifer, Jenny, Jessica, Jessy, Jillian, Joan, Joy, Joyce, Juanita, Judith, Judy, Jules, Julie, Justina, Karen, Kari, Kerry, Kate, Kat, Katherine, Kathy, Kathleen, Katie, Kay, Kim, Kimberly, Kimmy, Kirsten, Kristen, Kristina, Laura, Laurie, Leah, Leslie, Lilly, Lillian, Linda, Lisa, Lois, Louise, Lou-Ann, Loretta, Lorraine, Lori, Lucy, Lucille, Lynn, Madeline, Maggie, Mandy, Marcy, Margaret, Marge, Maria, Marian, Marie, Marilyn, Marlene, Marley, Marsha, Martha, Mary, Mary-Ellen, Melanie, Meg, Megan, Melissa, Meredith, Mirtha, Miriam, Mitzi, Monica, Monique, Myra, Nancy, Natalie, Nicky, Nicole, Nicolette, Nia, Norma, Noreen, Olivia, Olive, Pam, Pamela, Pat, Patrician, Paula, Pauline, Peg, Peggy, Penny, Phoebe, Phyllis, Priscilla, Rachel, Rebecca, Raine, Renee, Roberta, Robin, Rochelle, Rose, Rosalie, Rosalyn, Roxanne, Ruth, Sally, Samantha, Sandy, Sarah, Sasha, Sherry, Sharon, Sheila, Shirley, Sylvia, Shannon,

Shana, Sonia, Sophia, Stacey, Stephanie, Sue, Susan, Sue-Ellen, Suzannah, Tamara, Tammy, Teresa, Tess, Tia, Trisha, Trina, Vanessa, Veronica, Vicky, Victoria, Vivian, Wendy, Willow, Winnie, Zelda.

COMMON FIRST NAMES FOR MEN:

Aaron, Abe, Abraham, Adam, Al, Allen, Albert, Alex, Alfred, Alonzo, Alvin, Andrew, Andy, Angelo, Anthony, Archie, Armand, Arnold, Arthur, Austin, Barney, Barry, Baxter, Ben, Benjamin, Bernie, Bernard, Bert, Bill, Billy, Bob, Brad, Bradley, Bradford, Brandon, Brendon, Brian, Bruce, Bud, Byron, Carl, Carlos, Carter, Caesar, Cedric, Chad, Chandler, Charlie, Chet, Chuck, Chester, Chris, Christopher, Clark, Claude, Clayton, Cliff, Clint, Clyde, Cole, Collin, Conrad, Corey, Craig, Curt, Dallas, Danny, Daniel, Darren, Dave, David, Dennis, Den, Derek, Dexter, Dominick, Donald, Doug, Douglas, Drew, Duane, Dusty, Dwight, Earl, Ed, Eddi, Edward, Edgar, Edmund, Eli, Emmanuel, Eric, Ernie, Erwin, Ethan, Evan, Everette, Felix, Fletcher, Floyd, Frank, Francis, Fred, Frederick, Garrett, Gary, Geoffrey, George, Gerald, Gil, Gilbert, Graham, Grant, Greg, Gus, Hal, Hank, Hans, Harry, Harold, Hector, Henry, Herb, Howard, Hugh, Irving, Isaac, Ivan, Ivy, Jack, Jacob, Jake, James, Jason, Jay, Jerome, Jerry, Jeremy, Jessy, Joey, Joe, John, Jonathan, Johan, Jonah, Jordan, Joshua, Josh, Juan, Julio, Justin, Keith, Kenneth, Kenny, Kevin, Kirk, Kris, Kyle, Larry, Lawrence, Lee, Leonard, Leo, Leon, Leroy, Lou, Louie, Lucas, Lyle, Manny, Mark, Marvin, Mason, Matt, Matthew, Max, Melvin, Morris, Morgan, Nate, Nathan, Nick, Nicolas, Nicky, Noah, Noel, Norman, Otis, Ollie, Owen, Pat, Patrick, Paul, Pauly, Pedro, Peter, Phillip, Phil, Pierre, Preston, Ralph, Randy, Ray, Raymond, Richie, Rich, Rick, Richard, Robert, Robbie, Rob, Rodney, Roger, Rollin, Ronnie, Ronald, Rory, Ross, Russ, Russell, Samuel, Sammy, Scott, Sean, Shawn, Seymour, Steve, Stephen, Stewart, Stewie, Teddy, Terry, Theodore, Tom, Thomas, Timmy, Tim, Toby, Tobias, Todd, Tony, Tristan, Tyrone, Tyler, Victor, Vincent, Vinny, Wayne, Warren, Walter, William, Will, Wilbur, Xavier, Zack

Wow, talk about a long list of names. I bet you didn't think that there were that many different people in the world to be named after in the first place. Like I said earlier, this is just a rudimentary list of the most common first names for men and women in the US, it is not a complete list by any means. If there are other people in your life who have names that were included on this list, I again apologize and encourage you to write down their names in addition to what you have, and to come up with images that you can associate with such names. Now, the next most important thing to discuss is how to come up with images for each name that you have listed. Going back to what I said earlier about the **substitution method**, the main procedures used when trying to substitute one word for another or one name for another word, is to ask yourself what does the actual word either looks or sounds like.

Since we are using names that are associated with people you will possibly meet in real life situations, I think it would be a good start for now, to try to come up with images for how each individual name <u>sounds</u> like. For instance, when I hear the name "Florence" for a woman, I instantly think of a fence laying broken on the floor of a room (floor and fence combine to make Florence). Or if I met a man whose name was Vincent, I could picture a prince flipping a penny in the air (Prince sounds like Vince, and the penny in the air represent a cent, hence Vincent).

Now, the final step, which obviously takes a lot of imagination, is to be able to look at the person's face, find the distinguishing characteristic that grabs your attention (eyes, ears, nose, mouth, etc) and try to imagine that image <u>doing something to the person's face, as if in a short story</u>. This requires you to start with the focal point on the person's face, and to create a small "journey" around their face with the imaginary object. For example, with regards to the woman named Florence, let's say that this person had very red cheeks on their face. I could try to imagine a "fence" is covering her red cheeks and that the fence is falling off her face, down her jaw, and then to the "floor". This requires a few seconds of trying to look at other locations around the face, in order to create his odd yet imaginative journey about the person.

With regards to the gentleman named Vincent, let's say that this person has a receding grey hairline. Well, in this case, I would imagine a small crown atop a prince's head, as he is traveling up his hairline, and then a penny is popped into the air when the prince reaches the top. That is why I spoke to you earlier about looking at all of the contours of a human face from a photograph so that you can have a better idea about how to create a small story or journey along the locations of a human face.

In these instances, try to imagine imaginary lines or arrows traveling across the person's face from the focal point to another location on their face where their supposed "name" is supposed to stop. For instance, with regards to the name Florence, if the person has red cheeks and this reminds you of a fence, simply picture the fence spreading from one cheek to the other side of her face, and then imagine an arrow pointing down to the ground from her chin, symbolizing the floor. In the instance of the name Vincent, if the person's receding hair line reminds you for a prince with a crown on his head, try to envision an arrow pointing up his head towards the back of the skull, where the imaginary pennies are supposed to be popping up. By using such delineative lines or paths of direction on a person's face, you can literally make up a small story or comic strip occurring on the contours of the person's face, thereby giving you the entire name of the person.

However, before you start to get too happy or excited about your new creative ways of remembering other people's names, it is important to remember that you are actually trying to remember something about someone else that is very personal and very important. While it might be okay to divulge to others what you imagine or think about when you try to picture things like cards and numbers, **you should try to be careful about what images you reveal to them that remind you of various people's names**. I had one experience where I told a friend that the name "Otis" reminded me of a slobbering dog, only to later find out that this particular friends' late father was also named Otis, and he did not appreciate me disparaging his late father's first name. I could not help myself that such a name reminded me of one of my favorite comic characters.

But it was that experience that helped me to understand how sensitive people can be about their first names, especially if someone tries to make fun of their names. So, here is a word of caution for all you out there trying to improve your memories. **Please, do not reveal to anybody out there anything about what images or pictures you have created or imagined that could relate to various people's names in the world,** as you might accidentally offend someone and this will prove costly to you socially.

In order for you to get the chance to practice this exercise again in real life, I am going to be giving you a homework assignment that you can complete on your own. First, please continue to rehearse and go over all the related images that you have created for all the names that were both listed and any other ones that you came up with on your own. Second, make sure that you are prepared for the next social or formal gathering that is occurring in your personal life. And finally, when the day of such reunion finally comes, try to use the previous steps that were mentioned when you are with other people that you have either never met before or are unfamiliar with.

I guarantee you will be the life of the party when you are done with such occasion. When you get to the next social gathering of your choice, make sure to try to take a few seconds of your time and look at the other person's face (please don't stare as this is considered creepy). As you approach the person, continue to remind yourself of the Lucky 7 steps that were just mentioned, and then decide how you plan to go through with the steps yourself. When you meet the person you are looking at, give yourself a few seconds to focus on the individual focal point of their face that most interests you. When you are face to face with the person, just go through the steps and remember the image for their person's respective name, and then create the storyline for such image. This process in of itself should only take about 10-15 seconds at most. This will give you enough time to run through all the steps as you keep your eyes focused on the entire face, while also giving you the chance to get to know the person a little better.

Now, one question that you should ask yourself is what to do if the other person comes up from behind you and you did not expect to see them? Don't be too worried, just give yourself at least 3 more seconds time to look at the person's face and find a specific physical feature that intrigues your most, and then wait until the person actually gives you their name. However, if you are asked to come over and introduce yourself to <u>more than one person at a time</u>, this will make it very difficult to go through all the steps for each person without offending the others by making them wait to be spoken to. Instead, simply try to repeat the person's name in your head as fast you as can 3 times before you speak to the next person, it should only take about 5 seconds for each person. This way the name stays in your mind just long enough for you to go back and look through their faces again and start using the imaginary and storyline ideas when you have a chance to review your information later.

For your next assignment, I would like for you to try to remember the names and faces of at least **10 new people for every hour** that you are at such a function. You will probably not be able to allow yourself to walk across the room to greet all the people around you, as some individuals might really start to like you and begin chewing your ear off with conversation. Make it a point to try to give each person at least a few minutes of your time, and then move onto the next person while going through the steps and double checking your memory. I promise you, by the end of the evening, as long as you are diligent in going through the steps mentioned before, you should have no trouble remembering at least 25-30 people's names before the end of the affair. Once you are ready, go back and ask each person if you got their name right by walking over to them and saying "You said that your name was ___?

Continue to do this for each and every occasion when you have the chance, as you continue to work harder at trying to remember each person's name and face. You will then begin to see familiar faces come back into your life again, as they will be more recognizable than before, due to the fact that you had already taken the time to get to know them in the past. Watch what happens to your popularity that night and begin to finally discover, just like Jim Farley and Dale Carnegie already explained, about how beneficial and important it is to remember somebody else's name in conversation.

Chapter 10

Personal Data (tell me something about you)

When I was in high school, I remember my teacher giving us a catalog during our senior year, which was to be used to order our senior class rings. When I looked through the catalog, I made a few specific selections about what I was looking for and how I would like it to look. Afterwards, I sent in a check to the company and waited a few weeks for my order to come to the school. On the day that our rings finally arrived, there was a spokesperson from the company, who was sitting behind a table with the company logo in front of him. He also had a stack of order papers next to him, apparently receipts from all of the children that had ordered their rings from his company. He spent some time reading through each receipt and then placing them face down on a table.

When I finally put my ring on, it did not fit well and some of the designs were not correct. So naturally I wanted to complain about my level of services. When I was given the chance to stand in line to talk to him, I gave his assistant my name and account number and what my concerns were. Once I finally reached the front of the line and stated my last name out loud to him, he shocked me by later recalling my first and last name, as well as my address, my account number, and what my ring specifications were.

Needless to say, I was very impressed with this man's memory recall and his ability to make me feel unique and special, as opposed to just another person on that line who was there to harass him or waste his time. When the interview was done, he gave me back my money and I later reordered another ring according to my own specific tastes. This time, the ring came back a few days later in perfect condition, along with a note from the gentleman I had spoken to, expressing his apologies for the previous mistake. I realize now that if that person had treated like a just another number or a nameless creature that day, I would have never wanted to do business with him again, and probably would have been left the school with an angry feeling in my mind. (I should also point out that, on my high school ring, there is an emblem design that reads "Knowledge is power"). I realized then more than ever before just how important that particular slogan truly meant when it came to dealing with people and **personal data.**

As you probably know from my previous discussions with you, I do enjoy watching a lot of movies and referencing certain scenes from each picture to illustrate different important points for each of my chapters. With regards to remembering personal data, there was one movie that I saw back in early 1990 called "**A Few Good Men** that illustrates such a point. In that movie, the main character is a cocky, arrogant, and young, Harvard educated naval lawyer named Daniel Caffee, who has been recently assigned to take on a new case, and his immediate superior officer is a woman named Joanne Galloway, who does not always get along with him. During one scene, Joanne Galloway is talking to Daniel while he is outside playing a baseball game as opposed to being at his office and looking through job related paperwork. She does not seem impressed with his lack of concern for their clients or his less than professional work ethic as she states that she does not feel as though he is good enough to be the lawyer in charge of the case.

Daniel then counters against her by stating that "you don't even know me well enough". Once he eventually stops playing and later sits down, Joanne walks over to him, looks him right in the eyes and then recites his full name, his birthdate, the location of his birth, the name of his father and the jobs that his father had had, as well as where he himself went to school, and how long he has been in the Navy. At this point, Daniel is unable to speak and is in shock at her flawless recall of his biographical history. And it is only then, that he really starts to take her more serious and realize that she does in fact "know a lot more" about him than he realized.

Previously, we discussed in the last chapter how important it is to remember a person's name, and how guys such as Dale Carnegie and Jim Farley benefitted so greatly by recalling such information from the people that mattered the most in their lives. In this chapter, we are going to focus on how to learn to remember an **individual's personal information** and how to rehearse and recall such information when necessary. Unfortunately, there will be a lot more images and codes that need to be used in order to remember such information for later purposes (good news is that <u>you get to decide</u> what the codes will be), as most personal information cannot be classified the exact same way as names and numbers.

For this point of discussion, I am going to tell you the things that you already know from our previous discussions, and then I will give you more choices of what other information (again it is your choice if you want to learn such demographics) or personal data you can easily recall and how to do it. For now, let's talk about what <u>you already know</u> and then move onto to what you are about to learn. Be prepared, as this will probably be the longest chapter of the book, but also the most informative and comprehensive chapter of them all.

If you remember from our earlier chapters regarding how to memorize numbers, I asked you to come up with <u>100 different characters or images</u> for all numbers between **00-99**. As you may recall, each number is related to a different set up letters or initials that stand for the name of the person or character associated with each number. And whether you realize it or not, there are several bits of personal information about a person that can easily be recalled just by using numbers. So, guess what? Here is your first lesson on how to memorize a <u>person's birthdate, Social Security number and telephone number</u>, simply by using this system. And as you already know, such pieces of personal information like birthdays, Social Security and phone numbers can only be delineated by a random series of numbers. Therefore, this next lesson will be quite self-explanatory.

First, in order to remember a person's birthday, one thing that you should try to do is come up with an image that stands for the term "birth". I have two images in my mind that I can use interchangeably at any given time. I chose to either picture a baby in a thick blanket or a birthday party hat on a cake. Either one reminds me of the day that a person was born. You can come up with whatever images you would like for your own use. And for those of you who are familiar with a yearly calendar, you should probably already know the following order of the <u>12 months of the year</u>: January (**01**), February (**02**), March (**03**), April (**04**), May (**05**), June (**06**), July (**07**), August (**08**), September (**09**), October (**10**), November (**11**), and December (**12**). This way, in order to <u>picture the month</u> of the person's birthday, you would first start out by coming up with your own image for what a birthday represents, and then move onto the right side of that image, where you could attach the character for the corresponding month of the year which is listed in bold print.

As you are aware, the next piece of information would be <u>the day</u> of the month for such birthday, and you could attach another image for that number to the right side of the image of the month of birth. And then do the same thing for the year of birth, it is up to you if you want to use 4 digits for the year or just two. Let's say that your birthday is November 6th (don't worry about the year for right now). Then that image would correspond with the numbers 11/06, or the letters AA and OS. My characters for the numbers 11 and 06 are the Energizer bunny (11) and Oskar Schindler (06). And if I chose to use an image of a baby in a thick blanket, I could picture such baby lying on the ground and crying as there is a marching drum (AA) being strapped up to Oskar Schindler (OS) on his left side. And with that, you have now remembered the month and day of the person's birthday.

Also, if you are interested in trying to remember <u>certain days of the week</u>, be advised that there are only <u>seven days</u> in a week to have to remember. There are several different methods that you can come up with in order to recall such days if needed to when it comes to remembering birthdays. For instance, if you chose to remember Sunday as the first day of the week, you could think about Sunday as the number 01, and the corresponding image. In addition, you could also try to sound out each day of the week and try to come up with a substitute word for each image. I like to think of Sunday as a big, large sun, glowing down on me. Monday (01) is characterized by lots of money in my mouth, as this is usually when I cash my pay check. Tuesdays (02) is usually pictured as the Tooth Fairy wearing a tutu dress, hence the words repeat.

So, if you would like to try either strategy, feel free to use whatever method you are comfortable with when you are trying to connect important dates with the seven days of the week. So, if the birthday was July 27th and the day of week was Sunday, you could imagine the image for Sunday first, and then the characters for 07 and 27 to the right of such initial image. For this instance, I would first imagine a large sun (**Sunday**) beaming down on Oscar the Grouch (**07**) while he is trying to do some work on a lap top computer (**27**). (remember 27 is equal to BG, which stands for Bill Gates, I am simply using the PAO method again) And from there, you have a set of images to remind you of the day of the week for a person's birthday, as well as the actual birthdate itself.

In addition, if you are also wondering about how to remember certain times of the day, there is also a really good method for doing so, which I grew up learning early in my childhood. As I probably told you earlier, my late grandfather was very active in the Marine Corps, and as a child, he used to quiz me and my brother about how to read the actual time of the day in military time. For example, 3pm would be considered 15:00 hours, or fifteen hundred hours. This means that you would count the hours from midnight going forward, by simply adding the numbers as the hours continued on. 3am is 03:00 or 03 hundred hours, and 3pm would occur 12 hours later. Therefore, if you wanted to picture what 3pm looks like in terms of using your mnemonic images, you could easily picture your character or image for the number 15 (AE) with a large clock next to it. This lets you know what time of the day it is if you are interested in incorporating that into your personal data section.

Phone numbers and Social Security numbers are just as easy to do, as you can simply come up with another image for a phone and another image for Social Security. And then attach a series of pictures to the right side of either of these images in order to create a chain. (Remember from our discussion about setting the scene, where there is one character on the left and another to the right) For a telephone number, I can easily picture an old telephone ringing loudly. For Social Security, I can easily picture an old person with checks in their hands. And once that image is locked in, I just go about implanting any of my images to the right side of such introductory image. Remember, phone numbers are usually 7 digits long, unless you need to remember the area code as well, whereby it then become 10 digits long. Social Security numbers are only 9 digits long, so try to be careful how you organize your codes or images, as you don't want to recall too much information that is not needed. Be careful talking to strangers about this type of information, as you don't want to be at risk for identity theft or other related crimes.

Congratulations, now you know how to recall a person's birthdate, Social Security number and telephone number as well as days of the week and time of the day. I however cannot give out any personal information about myself or anybody else I know, and also would like to try to avoid accidently giving you any information about a person I have never met (sometimes you get lucky with putting together a bunch and numbers, and recognizing someone's else information). For now, just try out this lesson out on some people that you personally know or trust so that you can test your abilities to recall such information later on.

As stated earlier in the memory palace chapter, it would be beneficial to try to use your various memory palaces in a certain order so as to store such information in different rooms or areas of a room. Just be sure to remember to include the images associated with birthdays, Social Security and telephones as introductory images for each room. And if possible, try to start off in your memory palace by recalling the person's first and last name by using word associations. (in our previous chapter I told you to try to think of various images that you can use to substitute for a person's name). So, if I were to try to remember my aunt's birthday and phone number (I will never know her Social Security ever), I could easily picture her first and last name as two different images in the first room of my memory palace, then followed by images representing her birthday and day of the week in a second room, and other images representing her phone number in a third room, and so on. Now, I have some organizational tools needed in order to recall some basic information about an important person in my life.

Now, let us start to focus on the information that you <u>don't already know</u>. As you realize, there are endless different categories about personal information that apply to any given person. Some of it you can ascertain simply by talking to them, others items you will have to look up with investigative purposes. And all of the data can easily be stored in the other rooms or locations in any of your memory palaces. It is a good idea to try to use one memory palace for each individual person at a time, so that you don't get confused about other people's personal information.

But for now, the following topics or categories of personal information are going to be discussed: **addresses, foreign nationalities and ethnicities, vocational jobs, cars, family relations, hobbies, favorite foods, and educational degrees**. (don't worry, like I said, for these categories, you get to come up with your own images or codes, depending on whether you really want to remember such information or not). But by being able to do this type of memory challenge, you will be able to effectively recall at least **<u>12 different pieces of personal information</u>** just for one individual person. Imagine the look on their face when you recall back such information to them accurately and effortlessly, they will think that you have their entire biography listed in your head (remember, <u>knowledge</u> is not just power, <u>knowledge</u> is **PEOPLE** power).

With regards to **addresses**, it is quite easy to recall the actual number of the residential household or the zip code of the town that a person lives in, simply by just using your previously <u>100-character codes</u> for numbers. However, when it comes to remembering the actual <u>street</u> and <u>state</u> for such address, here are some ideas and suggestions to use in order to help recall such residential information more accurately. First, I will present to you a list of the <u>50 states of the United States of America</u>. As you remember from your past chapter on word memory, I would like to give you your first assignment for this chapter, by coming up with <u>an associated image or character</u> for each of the **50 states** listed below so that you can easily recall such image later.

As far as how I have done it, I usually try to think of either how the name of the state actually sounds or something very iconic or famous about the state itself. I am from New York, so I can easily picture either a Big Apple or the Twin Towers. As for maybe Hawaii, I can picture a volcano or a hula girl dancing. Other states might require some more thought and imagination. For now, just try to think of an image that either sounds like, looks like, or is historically associated with for each state, and write that information next to each name of the states listed below.

Alabama	Montana
Alaska	Nebraska
Arizona	Nevada
Arkansas	New Hampshire
California	New Jersey
Colorado	New Mexico
Connecticut	New York
Delaware	North Carolina
Florida	North Dakota
Georgia	Ohio
Hawaii	Oklahoma
Idaho	Oregon
Illinois	Pennsylvania
Indiana	Rhode Island
Iowa	South Carolina
Kansas	South Dakota
Kentucky	Tennessee
Louisiana	Texas
Maine	Utah
Maryland	Vermont
Massachusetts	Virginia

Michigan	Washington
Minnesota	West Virginia
Mississippi	Wisconsin
Missouri	Wyoming

I am sure that you realize that there is no way I can possibly expect you to come up with images for all the major towns, cities, and villages for each and every state in this country (now that would be a seriously major large assignment). As far as how to recall the actual name of any city, town or village, simply use the same substitute word system as before with the US states. Just ask yourself what the name of the location actually sounds or looks like, or if you know something personal about such district. As for me, I currently work in Middletown, so I can easily think of something that reminds me of the word "middle" or perhaps something else related to the high school's team logo. You would then attach that image to the left side of the image for any of the states, and then just add the zip code to the end of it.

As far as the actual street address is concerned, continue to use the same substitute word system as before. However, if you would like to create your own mnemonic images for the **actual types of US road designations** that are currently in use, I have included a list of such names if you would like to use this as a reference in regarding addresses. Chose whatever images come to mind when you hear or see any of these following words. I have included several images that I personally use for each type of travel route.

TYPE OF ROADWAY	ASSOCIATED IMAGE
Alley	Alley cat
Avenue	Van with new sign in window
Boulevard	Large bull in a yard
Bi-Way	Ocean waves crashing
Causeway	Santa Clause on moving sleigh
Court	Legal court room
Drive	Automatic car stick shift

Highway	Toll booths
Interstate	Innerspace movie space ship
Lane	Yellow lines on road
Road	Concrete blocks
Route	Compass on GPS machines
Park	Swing set
Terrace	Terrorist cell
Way	Arms waving

So, rather than going on to the following topic of personal data, let's try to visualize an example of a person's actual address, including their residential house number, city and state. One such person that I truly like to use as an example is the president of the United States, Donald Trump (we all know what he physically looks like, so the imagery should be very easy for this). Okay, so if I wanted to remember not only his face, but also his actual work address (the White House address is **1600 Pennsylvania Avenue in Washington DC 20500**), I would picture his name and face in the first room of my memory palace. Then I could picture the numbers (16) and (00), which stand as the letters AS and OO. Accordingly, in my system, these characters are represented as Arnold Schwarzenegger (AS) and James Bond (OO).

Therefore, in the next room of my memory palace, I could picture Arnold drinking from a martini glass while shooting a gun from a concealed pocket, just like James Bond. This would give me the numbers 1600. And then on his right side, I could imagine the image that I have for the state of Pennsylvania, which is a pencil sharpener with lots of pencils coming out of it. And then next to this image on the right hand side, would be another character that would represent the word Avenue, which for me, is a van with a new sign posted in its front window. So, I could see a large pencil sharpener with lots of pencils, drilling themselves into the front sign of an old van into a street.

Then in the next room or possibly the following location (depending on how big your rooms are in your memory palace), I could imagine a character for the city <u>Washington</u>, which is simply just an image of a washing machine with lots of clothes coming out of it. Next to the right of that figure are the letters <u>DC</u>, and such letters will always pertain to the associated character for the number <u>43</u>, which is usually Dick Clark. So, I will imagine a washing machine loaded with lots of clothes, while Dick Clark is standing next to it, trying to pull a largely lighted New Year's Eve ball from inside of it (goofy images are the easiest to remember).

Finally, when it comes to the zip code, I can easily picture the images for the following numbers, <u>20-50</u>, or (BO) and (EO). The letters BO represent for me, our former president Barack Obama, and the letter EO represent comic actor Ed O'Neill from Married with Children. Therefore, standing to the right side of Dick Clark, would be an image of Barack Obama (20) putting women's shoes on his own feet (50), while standing near a large hole (0). And there you have it, the **entire address** for the White House, in just several different associated images, linked from left to right, in different rooms or different locations within each room of one of your memory palaces.

With regards **to foreign nationalities or ethnicities**, I have always found that people are always very happy when you pay attention to them enough to get to know a little bit more about their ancestry, as it lets them know that you appreciate who that person is and where they have come from. We all attach some deep personal pride and respect to our nationalities simply because, like our own names, this characteristic will also be with us all the way until our death. Now, I do not know exactly how many actual different nationalities there are in the world, but I have attached a list of the <u>50 most common nationalities</u> that I have seen currently in the United States. (if I have excluded or forgotten to include your own personal nationality or heritage, I apologize deeply as I cannot come up with images for every single nationality in the world). For now, here is another list of the <u>50 most common nationalities in the US.</u> Feel free to come up with any images for any nationality that you feel comfortable with.

So, if I wanted to think about an image for the nationality of

Italian, I could picture an image of the Leaning Tower of Pisa, with a large pizza smothered on top of it. And if I wanted to remember that one of my relatives was Italian, which most of them usually are, I could picture the name and face of one of my relatives standing alongside this creative image for the nationality of Italy. (like I said, if you don't want to create images or try to remember a person's nationality for personal reasons, that is entirely up to you, I am giving you a reference list to use at a later date). Also, try not to share with people how you came up with such images for nationalities or ethnicities, as you don't want to insult or upset such person by telling them that their nationality reminds you of an obscure scene or object. (remember the lesson from name memory in regards to avoiding hurting other people's feelings)

Afghan	Indian
Amish	Iraqi
Arab	Irish
Austrian	Israeli
Australian	Italian
Belgian	Jamaican
Bosnian	Japanese
Brazilian	Jerusalem
Cambodian	Korean
Chinese	Louisiana Creole
Colombian	Mexican
Cuban	Native American
Czech	Norwegian
Danish	Pakistani
Dominican Republic	Polish
Dutch	Puerto Rican
Egyptian	Portuguese
English	Russian
Finnish	Scottish
French	Somali

German	Spanish
Greek	Swedish
Haitian	Turkish
Hispanic	Venezuelan
Hungarian	Vietnamese

Interestingly, one of the most common and popular questions that I get asked by other people, who are just trying to get to know me and make small talk, is the usual question of **what I do for a living**. (As you may recall earlier, I mentioned that I am a *clinical social worker*). But what if the person has absolutely no idea what that term actually means or what field of vocation you actually practice in? In this new day and age, there are so many different types of job titles, positions, and designations out there that most of us just simply shake our heads when we hear what other people do for a living, and are just thankful that they have a job in the first place. However, if you don't understand what field of employment a person generally has, here is another list of the **25 most common fields of vocational employment** in the US.

So even though you might not be able to recall exactly what a person does for a living, at least you will make them feel better by remembering what field or specialty they practice within. So for me, my field of work is listed in the section labeled <u>Community and Social Services</u>. And for that, I could easily picture a person handing out bread to the homeless at a food shelter. (Again, feel free to come up with any related images or character that you can think for each field of practice, as most of the jobs mentioned are so common nowadays, that we might already know somebody or someone that is employed within them).

Architecture and Engineering
Arts, Design, Entertainment, Sports, and Media
Building and Grounds Cleaning and Maintenance
Business and Financial Operations
Community and Social Services
Computers and Mathematical sciences
Construction and Extraction
Education, Training, and Library
Farming, Fishing, and Forestry
Food/drink Preparation and Serving Related
Healthcare/medical Practitioners and Technical
Healthcare Support staff
Installation, Maintenance, and Repair
Legal, correctional, law enforcement
Military or Armed Services
Life, Physical, and Social Science
Management, entrepreneur, or administration
Office and Administrative Support
Personal Care and Home Service
Production of products
Private Business store owner
Protective Services
Private practice employment
Sales and Related products
Transportation and Material Moving

I don't know about you, but I for one always enjoy commenting or bragging about **what type of automobile** I drive or used to own in the past. For many people, owning a car is like owning a new part of oneself. Sometimes the car defines you, other times it tends to categorize you. That is why, if I meet a person who is driving a nice new automobile, one of the first things I like to ask them is what is the make and model of the car. (I do not know much about cars, but sometimes just acknowledging what a person drives is a compliment in of itself). Therefore, I have attached a list of the <u>35 most common brands of vehicles</u> that have been made in the past decade (if I have left any out, I again apologize as I am only going by personal experience, and don't always know people that have owned newer and more advanced vehicles). Here is a list of the **35 most common brands of vehicles** if you would like to create any images for such. (by the way, if you are into selling or manufacturing cars as a job, this area of memory is a gold mine for you).

Acura	Kia
Aston Martin	Lamborghini
Audi	Land Rover
Bentley	Lexus
BMW	Lincoln
Buick	Maserati
Cadillac	Mazda
Chevrolet	Mercedes
Chrysler	Mini
Dodge	Porsche
Ferrari	Ram
Fiat	Rolls Royce
Ford	Saab
Honda	Subaru
Hyundai	Suzuki
Infiniti	Toyota
Jaguar	Volkswagen
Jeep	Volvo

Sometimes, when I am introduced to a stranger by someone else that I already know, the first thing I start to wonder about is, how does this person know the individual that I am already familiar with? Are they a friend, family, co-worker, neighbor, or some other relation? When I was younger, I used to look at my **own family tree** and wonder how each person was related to another, as there was no major key or legend that was used to delineate each relationship to each other. In mental health, it is a common practice to create what is known as a family **genograph**, which is a picture of the client's name in the center of the page, followed by a bunch of other names with various symbols around such name, defining the types of relationships between all listed persons.

However, in the real world, that is not always possible as most of us don't walk around with a sheet of paper when we talk to others. Therefore, if you have the lucky chance to get to look at another person's family tree or just want to get a general idea of the family composition at an upcoming social gathering, here is a list of the **25 most common relationship statuses** that exist among most people in the US. Try to think of a concrete image that you can associate with each relationship status and get ready to be able to know an entire family tree by heart.

Father
Mother
Brother
Sister
Stepmother
Stepfather
Stepbrother
Stepsister
Grandfather
Grandmother
Aunt
Uncle
Cousin
Niece
Nephew
Daughter
Son
Grandchild
Friend/Neighbor
In Law
Colleague
Wife
Husband
Fiancée
Ex-spouse

Perhaps the easiest question to ask a person in a causal conversation is about what likes or dislikes or interests the person has. This will usually lead to a very long and verbose conversation if the person is comfortable in talking to you. When it comes **to hobbies, recreational activities, and favorite foods**, this is usually the easier topic to memorize, as you only have to just picture the activity or food itself, or something related to either one. If you have never heard of the particular activity or food, simply just ask the person to either clarify it for you or ask them how it is either spelled. This will help you to be able to visualize it in your head and place it in another room of your memory palace. So if the person likes eating pasta, skiing or collecting stamps, simply just imagine someone actually doing any of these activities in another room of your memory palace. If the person likes eating pasta or pizza, simply picture such food items in another room of your memory palace in the same way.

As far as **educational degrees** are concern, don't worry about trying to recall exactly what the actual field of study of the person involved is, or the exact words for their educational degree (I have a master's degree in social work, however just remembering that I have a master's degree in the field of mental health is usually good enough, as some people do not know exactly what social work is). The only thing that we are going to be covering in this section is what <u>exact level of education</u> the person truly has, not what they studied or where they studied. As far as knowing what areas of study the person has worked on, or what institution they graduated from, that could take up a lot of time and paper in this book as there are literally thousands and thousands of schools throughout the US as well as hundreds of different high school and college related major fields of study. However, if you really want to recall the actual level of education that the person actually has, the one thing that you have not yet learned is to create a mnemonic image for the letter **M**. I will tell you why in just a moment.

When it comes to receiving educational in the US, there are only a few degrees that can be received from institutions of higher learning; <u>high school, community college, bachelor level college, graduate school, or doctoral school.</u> In this case, the letter **M** would relate to someone with a *master's* degree and **D** would relate to someone with a doctorate or PhD if you want to use that term. (MSW stands for Masters in Social Work, by the way). You probably already have an image for the letter D as it can be represented by the number 04. As for me, the letter **M** is the first initial of my brother's name, so I can easily picture him. Remember earlier when you were coming up with images for <u>your 100 number characters or persons</u>; well, it looks as though some of the letters that you used to correlate with some of those numbers just happen to appear on the list below. So, if you think about it, if you were someone who has a high school (HS) degree, that would translate to the number 86, which is my character of Han Solo. If you have an associate's degree in the science of any related subject, then that would be the letters AS or 16, which is my image for Arnold Schwarzenegger.

Also, if the person did not finish high school, simply ask them <u>what grade level</u> they last finished, and just remember the actual <u>number</u> for that grade. Below are the following types of educational degrees that can be earned from going to school in the US. And if you can combine this imagery with the information regarding **what field of work or vocation** the other person is involved in, then you can easily ask somebody a question that sounds like "I know that you have a <u>master's</u> degree in the field of <u>social services</u>, am I correct? You could remember this information by placing the face and name of such person in one of your memory palace rooms, followed closely next to images for the actual subject of *social services*, and then the image for the letter *M*. That would be good enough for me if we met up during a causal occasion anywhere, as I would take it as a compliment that you remembered such information about me.

<u>Grades 1-12=</u>	associated letters (OA, OB, OC, OD, etc)
<u>GED=</u>	**General Educational Degree (754)**
<u>HS-</u>	**High School graduate (86)**
<u>AS-</u>	**Associates in the science of (16)**
<u>AA-</u>	**Associates in the arts of (11)**
<u>BS-</u>	**Bachelors in the science of (26)**
<u>BA-</u>	**Bachelors in the arts of (21)**
<u>MA-</u>	**Masters in the arts of**
<u>MS-</u>	**Masters in the science of**
<u>DA-</u>	**Doctorate in the arts of (41)**
<u>DS-</u>	**Doctorate in the science of (46)**

Additionally, it also does not hurt to try to remember **important historical events from a person's life** in the exact order that they came in. Ordinarily, we would likely assume that the first thing that ever happened to a person involved their actual birth (unless you are someone named Benjamin Button, watch the movie) So, with regards to a person's autobiography, if you wanted to remember a persons' birthday as being the first piece of information to enclose in your memory palace, you would place it in the first room of such palace. Then you could move forward and start remembering other important details such as their immediate birth family relations, then move on to other things such as where they grew up, when they went to school, and other things like jobs, marriage and children. Remember that scene I described earlier from the movie A Few Good Men, where Joanne Galloway recites all of the personal information about Daniel Kaffee.

Well, in that scene, she started off first by recalling his birthday, then proceeded next with the location of where he was born, followed by remembering what his father's name was, then later the name of school where Daniel had gone to study, and finally his current job in the navy. By saying all of the information in that particular order, you are literally reciting a person's <u>short personal biography</u> back to them. Just wait and see the look in someone's eyes when you are able to recite their own individual short story back to them in such a way as this, they won't know what to say in return.

Below I have attached a list of **6 major types of personal events** that can occur to the average person in their lifetime; please feel free to make up whatever images or characters you would like for each type of event so as to use them as reference points for organizing your autobiographical materials. Remember earlier when I said that my image for a birthday is a baby in a blanket. Well, I could also picture a wedding dress to symbolize a wedding, or a formal suit to symbolize a job. You will probably see some of these mentioned in the future chapter on book memory (remember, autobiographical information is also similar to book information)

BIRTHDAY=
AREAS OF RESIDENCE=
MARRIAGE DATE=
CHILDREN BORN=
JOB RECEIVED=
SCHOOL GRADUATED=

So, in closing, I would like to say that, if you can combine all of these memory topics along with a person's name, then you will have a grand total of **12 pieces of personal information** about the person that you can recollect at any given time. I use this process on a lot of my clients, as I am also privy to lots of their personal health information. When I first greet a client for the initial appointment, I already have glanced through their file and have created my own personal mental "Farley File", with the previously mentioned 11 topics, including their name. I like to refer to this technique as the "**Loving Dozen technique**" (a play on the words for the movie The Dirty Dozen, another favorite movie of mine, as well as the rhyming sounds of both words). So, once I meet with a new client, after I have recite back the name of the person, I then go on to recall the other 11 personal related facts about them, one at a time. Once I am done, that person will usually be very astonished by my memory recall, and will most often chose to remain with me as their primary clinician.

Just imagine how well this could work for you in the real world, when it comes to either making new friends (don't expect to get any information regarding Social Security's numbers though due to identity theft), going on a date after online chatting, getting along better with colleagues, being the life of the party, or just simply trying to attract that new client or customer at work that could help you land a great commission sale. This Loving Dozen technique is guaranteed to make the other person feel worthwhile and special around you, as they realize that you took the time and energy needed to get to know several of the most important topics in their lives. I will give you an exercise on a more condensed version of this technique later on in the chapter. But for now, give it a try sometime and see what happens in your social life or your job performance reviews, I promise that you will walk away with a renewed sense of confidence and charisma.

Earlier in the chapter, I spoke to you about an incident that occurred to me when I was a teenager, where my high school class ring did not match the exact specifications that I had asked for. My particular complaint was about the quality of the product itself, and fortunately the person in charge of purchasing already knew this information and was able to effectively handle my particular situation. Don't forget about what I said earlier regarding the famous self-help author Dale Carnegie, because being able to classify the <u>type of problem that a customer is having</u> is also extremely vital in being able to know how to address such person effectively, as opposed to just remembering their personal information. Each conflict has its own way of being resolved, as long as the professional in charge knows exactly what the problem actually it. This gives such individual a starting point in terms of knowing where to begin with such areas of conflict management.

For those of you who are interested in how to better deal with customer complaints and issues with client satisfaction, there is one more scale that I have devised on my own, that can be used in a similar fashion in order to better deal with such unfortunate business dilemmas. I have composed together a list of the **13 most common types of customer complaints** that most companies through the US regularly deal with. The hard part about this particular memory strategy is the ability to categorize individual complaints into different yet comprehensive descriptions. And for that, I have simplified each customer complaint to include a generalized description for each concern.

I have also included a list of several related images that I personally tend to use to try to recall each type of customer complaint so that I am better prepared to know what type of intervention to use with each particular person before I meet with them. Please feel free to use whatever images you prefer for yourself in regards to each category, but for now here is a list of the **13 most common customer or client related complaints** encountered in the US business world. (remember, **13** is an <u>unlucky</u> number, so this will help a little bit in being able to recall such information if needed).

COMPLAINT TYPE	RELATED IMAGE
Waiting too long in line for help or assistance	Long line of people standing together
Bureaucratic phone transfers from line to line	Old phone switchboard machine with wires
Lack of support from others or neglect of care	Person starving in a homeless cardboard box
Fault product or loss of money due to purchase	Broken dish next to a piggy bank
Complaint or problem not resolved by others yet	Person with palms praying in the air
No call back or contact from company	Old style rotary phone on table
Poor company reputation	Trophy in a trophy case
Product service delivery problem	Package box at door step
Employee behavior or lack of professionalism	Jester with bruises on face
Misunderstanding of client compliant	Bullseye with arrow piercing through
Product too expensive	Large pile of money
Confused about company hierarchy/management	Broken ladder with chain wrapped on it
Uncertain of how to resolve problem itself	Road map with question marks on it

Before you go, for those of you who would like to see if the previously mentioned Loving Dozen technique really works, or for those of you who want to actually use it in the real world, I have enclosed one exercise that I would like to test you on in order to determine how well you can use this Loving Dozen technique. Below, I have included fictional information about 4 fictional people (these are not real people and their information is completely made up). I have chosen not to use last names, as it would be easier to test you on just first names for now.

Below each name are <u>11 different fictional personal facts</u> about each person, written in four different columns. The topics are the person's name, address, phone number, Social Security number, nationality, occupation, personal car, relationship status, favorite hobbies, favorite foods, and educational degree. You were tested on all of these areas previously in the chapter.

You will need two sheets of paper to do this exercise. On the first sheet, write out all the information as it is listed in the chart structure below. Then, once you are done writing all the information out, simply read through each person's personal information and then try to use the previously mentioned techniques to memorize it. For this exercise, once you are done writing out the information, I am giving you <u>exactly 30 minutes</u> to look through all of the information for <u>all four people</u>. (that means there are 48 different pieces of personal information total). Then flip that page over, and use the other sheet of paper to record your answers. You can give yourself <u>2 points for each correct answer (grand total of 96</u>). If you can memorize it all in under 30 minutes, give yourself <u>an extra 4 points</u> to make it an even 100. (try to record your time as well if possible).

Please continue to practice this exercise at least once a day for one week and see how well you do at the end of the week. Don't worry too much about getting it right the first time because most people usually cannot do it so easily. Just see how much easier and faster it is for you to recall at the end of 7 days, and then you will begin to realize just how effective this could be for you in your personal life. Dale Carnegie and Jim Farley were both right about these concepts as it worked well for both of them. Now see if it can work the same magic for you. Good luck, nice getting to *know* you (haha)

John	Jane	Jack	Jill
March 11, 1991	June 13, 1992	May 4, 1969	September 29, 1977
23 Main Street, Happytown, UT 20973	47 Parrots Way, Funnyville, HA 90773	1564 Pond Park, Sillyberg, WY 63944	6767 Cloudy Terrace, Boringtown, VT 23390
(478) 964-5558	(854)832-4446	(254) 465-8870	(650) 061-5539
SS# 27-085-9982	SS# 85-001-4653	SS# 380-88-7722	SS# 115-90-7667
Italian and Irish	French and Spanish	German and Polish	Mexican and Austrian
Teacher/ Professor	Secretary	Car Salesman	Police Officer
Black Toyota	Blue Mercedes	Red Pick-up Truck	Purple Subaru
Husband	Wife	Aunt	Older brother
Sailing, hiking, golf	Collects stamps + coins	Volleyball + art books	Guitar and piano
Pasta, steak, eggs	Garden salads and fruit	Rice and beans	Fruit and yogurt
PHD	AA	BS	MS

DAY EXERCISE	SCORE (PERCENT/ CORRECT)	TIME (MINUTES, SECOND)
FIRST DAY		
SECOND DAY		
THIRD DAY		
FOURTH DAY		
FIFTH DAY		
SIXTH DAY		
SEVENTH DAY		

CHAPTER 11

Poems and speeches

When I was in high school, I remember our English teacher telling us that, for our junior year mid- term exam, we were going to be quizzed on Shakespeare's epic love story, "<u>Romeo and Juliet</u>". Now, I personally loved the actual story as well as the movie itself, as well as the condensed or simplified version of this tragic drama. However, when it came to trying to read and verbally rehearse the parts line for line, I found myself literally "tongue tied" and unable to comprehend, much less memorize what I was actually saying. I was afraid that I would fail one of my most important exams that year just because I could not understand the composition of something that was written in a language that I already spoke.

It was then that I first heard about Shakespeare himself having used a different version of the memory palace himself within the walls of his own bard, where he used to host his plays. He would imagine certain scenes for each part of his plays, and then would be able to recall all the words and sounds, and then pronounce them perfectly during some of his pre-play auditions along with his fellow staff. And I thought, well, if he could do it, perhaps other people like me should be able to do it as well.

As you probably remember from the earlier part of his book, I used an example for how to memorize several pieces of information together, going from left to right, with one figure connecting to another in a sequence. We referred to this procedure as "setting the scene". Nothing could be more relevant to memorizing poetry, as being able to set the "<u>stage</u>" figuratively in your mind so that you can remember the actual words and phrases of a poem. Going back to the very beginning of the book, there were a lot of famous movies that I used to watch as a child that initially inspired my interest in the field of memory.

When I was older, I came to realize that, for most actors and actresses on the silver screen, there was always a lot of pressing need to have to memorize lines so that such entertainer could give a great performance while on camera. Otherwise, if the actor could not memorize their lines accordingly, such person would end up sounding too robotic or unsure of themselves during performances. There were no teleprompters or large cue cards that the actors could use during their actual live performances as this would cause them to have to look away at times in order to read their lines. If the actors did read their lines during a performance, this would result in that person either getting distracted or making the scene itself look completely unbelievable. Either way, memorizing lines, as well as poetry, has proved to be a vitally important skill needed for someone who is hoping to become a great Hollywood actor or actress in this modern age.

With that being said, let us start to figure out how we can use the memory palace, or the link method, to help us in recalling large strings of words in our heads, without spending too much time repeating them over and over to make sure that they "stick". First, as you will recall from the previous chapter on word or vocabulary memory, in order to remember a long list of words, it is necessary for you to picture each word, one at a one, with a different visual image in your head, and then attach those images to a certain point or location in one of your memory palaces.

However, be advised that most of the words that I gave you earlier to recall in the vocabulary section, were simply nouns (persons, object and places). If you are going to recall poetry or lines of a speech correctly, you will have to be able to recall other types of words such as verbs and adjectives. However, as easy as it is to remember a noun, which is something that you can either see or hear, how does one go about recalling something as arbitrary or ambiguous as a verb or an adjective? That is where I seemed to fall apart during my youthful days in high school, as I had no problem remembering the actual nouns, but would suddenly fall short when it came to memorize different kinds of words.

Probably the easiest way to be able to perform this task, is the use of the age-old method, that was described earlier in the name and faces memory chapter, referred to as the substitution method. As you might remember, when you had to try to recall a person's name and attach an image to their face, one of the first things you needed to ask yourself was what exactly that person's name reminded you of. In order to memorize either verbs or adjectives, one of the best ways to do so, at least for myself, is to ask yourself, what does that word either look like or sound like?

So, with that in mind, below you will see a list of some common verbs, or words that describe actions, detailed below (by the way, I am an animal lover, so these are the only verbs that my parents' dog has ever been trained to obey). When you look at the verb, ask yourself if you could visualize an image for such action and if you could attach such image itself to another noun. For example, if think of the verb "run", and the noun that precedes it is the word "dog", I could easily picture a dog running through a field. If I picture the word "play" and the noun that precedes it is a "child", I can just picture a child playing on a swing set. Most verbs can be easily discerned and memorized once you understand the context of the sentence or situation.

Run
Jump
Hide
Play
Sit
Lay down
Turn around
Catch
Stay
Move

For most of us, this task seems relatively easy, as these are very common action verbs. And with the previously mentioned reference to a family dog or a child, is it not that difficult to visualize an animal, or a person if need be, doing any of these listed actions. So, when you see an action verb listed in a sentence, take a moment and ask yourself what does that word truly mean in of itself? Then, if it is still too difficult to come up with an image for such action verb, then try to picture the actual word occurring in the context of a story and use the substitution method as needed by asking yourself what the word really looks like or sounds like. I will give you another list of verbs underneath this paragraph that are not as easy to visualize in terms of images or pictures, but trust me, they are all real common verbs that are used in sentences.

Communicate
Detect
Forbid
Enunciate
Assemble
Organize
Delineate
Prepare

Now, I bet that was not as easy as learning the verbal commands needed for training a dog, huh? Well, that is okay, because most verbs are not as easy to visualize as some other straightforward terms. As you will see below, I have listed the same other verbs for you to memorize that are not the same as the first list. However, before you start feeling overwhelmed, let me tell you how I actually try to remember these particular terms, and see if you can either follow along with me, or come up with a similar yet different method of your own. Here are some examples of the previously mentioned verbs, and just how I actually try to visualize the real meanings behind these common yet ambiguous vocabulary verbs.

Communicate- I picture Ronald Reagan answering a telephone (he was known as the Great Communicator)

Detect- I picture Sherlock Holmes with a magnifying glass, with ticks all over it, and coming to some conclusion.

Forbid- I picture a person with four bids on their shirt, waving their finger at you to stay away from them

Enunciate- I picture a nun (nun) going into the CIA (cia) headquarters

Assemble- I picture a group of people being huddled together near a large copy of the Bill of Rights (first amendment is the right to assemble)

Organize- I picture a group of musical organs, with eyeballs on them.

Delineate-I picture a deli market (deli) with a person cleaning it up inside, saying that it is neat (neat)

Prepare- I always think of the Boy Scout image or icon (I am an Eagle Scout by the way)

Do you see how that works? As compared to actually trying to mentally go over and over the same word, hoping that the words stay in your mind, this is far more guaranteed to work. Granted, I do not have an actual list of all of the actual vocabulary verbs in the English dictionary along with any corresponding images for my memory. (as this would take a lot of time and paper to accomplish). But what I do is simply take just a few seconds and look at the word, and then either try to break it up into at least two parts (look at the section earlier about how to remember prefixes if you want to use that as a reference) or I just ask myself what the word really looks like or sounds like.

This can take a little more time than it would take to be able to remember a vocabulary word such as a noun, or an easy verb. But this process does give you brain the chance to expand its creativity and continue to enhance your visualization skills as well. It should be much easier for you to connect a noun and a verb together in your mind, and then place such images in different locations of your memory palace. Now, let's try to memorize both lists of verb words back to back in one of your memory palaces. First, you would start off with the word "run" and then proceed onto the word "jump". Use either your memory palace or the number associations for first and second word order if you would like. Give yourself about two minutes on this exercise to see how well you can visualize abstract wording.

However, before you start to think that the same type of advice can be applied to memorizing actual texts or sentences, let me give you some much easier and more simplistic advice that you probably already know. There are several steps that need to be taken in order to better memorize poetry or speeches in general. In order to effectively **memorize a line of poetry**, or a sentence from a speech, one of the first things that you must do is actually <u>read through the line itself</u>. Go ahead and read the poem or speech to yourself and try to understand what the actual story really is about. Do this at least twice in order to better comprehend what it is you are reading.

Once you are done doing this, then try to figure out what the story is trying to tell you (we each have our own definition of what we read, no one is the same). This will help you to decide what types of images or characters you would like to include in your memory palace as opposed to others. For example, with regards to Romeo and Juliet, as most of us know, this play takes place over hundreds of years ago in a small village in Italy. For anyone that has seen the play or the movie, we all know what the characters were dressed like and what the characters sounded like. Therefore you could pick images in your mind for either nouns or verbs that were somewhat related to the theme of this great play.

The next step you can take once you are familiar with the theme of the poem or speech is to determine if the information itself rhymes or if there is some type of pattern or pentameter to the actual wording. Some poems and speeches are designed to have a certain number of "<u>beats</u>" or <u>syllables</u> in each line, letting you know just how long each particular is expected to be. Try to count out this number silently on your fingers as you go through each sentence, and you will more than likely be entertained by the rhythm. This can be very good to know when you want to be prepared for how much information (or how many images) you would like to place in any location or room in your palaces. And even if the poem or speech does not have a style or pattern to it, don't be surprised if the number of words or ideas is very similar for each sentence, as this shows pattern organization in vocabulary.

Finally, after you have taken these <u>first</u> <u>two steps</u>, the only thing left to do would be to <u>copy the first line of speech or the poem</u> word for word, on a separate sheet of paper, without looking at the original. Keep the original copy on one side of you, and the newer page on a different side of you. Make sure to use a pencil for the writing as it is easier to either erase or change your answers. Once you are done with the first sentence, go back and see what parts of it you were not able to easily recall, and ask yourself what you could do to better remember such missing information later. Then, put the original copy away for a few seconds, and try memorizing the first line a second time, and see how much better you did.

After this, try to repeat the same pattern for the second line of the original, and then the third and the fourth line, until you are done with the first paragraph. Once you have repeated this process for the first paragraph, give yourself a minute to relax. And then see if you can remember the entire first paragraph exactly word for word on the separate sheet of paper in just one sitting. You will be amazed as how accurate your recall is. And even if you missed either one or two words throughout the entire paragraph, you will see that your recall is much greater than it ever was before.

So, say for example you wanted to remember a particular speech using these same steps, such as the <u>Gettysburg address</u>. You would want to phrase the speech in the following way. The first line of the speech goes like this: "***Four score and seven years ago our fathers brought forth on this continent, a new nation, conceived in Liberty, and dedicated to the proposition that all men are created equal***". In this instance, you could try to picture something that resembles the number "<u>four</u>", then picture something else that reminds you of the word "<u>score</u>", followed by the image for <u>07</u> and something else for the word "<u>years</u>". Try to only do a few words at a time for each room in your memory palace, as you will only have a certain amount of room to place most of the information. You could also try to remember the speech by dividing the sentence into different parts, such as 4 or 5 words at a time, and then place each sequence of images for such words into different rooms of the memory palace.

You can also choose to use the link method by attaching the number of the corresponding sentence to match the related images that you had created earlier for the number's memory chapter. (first line equal 01 or OA, second line equals 02 or OB, etc). Then attach the story to the rest of the line. For example, the character that you made up for number 01 or OA, would be on the left side in your field of vision, followed by the rest of the images linking up on the right side of such. You can also do this for regular lines of text in a book or on a page, simply by putting numbers alongside the left of each sentence, and then proceeding the same way. Either way is up to you, however, using this method you will only get up to 100 lines at a time, and will have to wait before you try to use them again in order to avoid the chalk board phenomenon mentioned earlier.

The last thing to try to work on for the purposes of memorizing poetry or speeches is something that we see very day but usually don't pay much attention to. And that can be summed up in two words: punctuation marks. Things like periods, commas, quotation marks and other related images are things that we see all the time in English grammar, yet it seems next to impossible to remember them as opposed to actual vocabulary words. However, for anybody out there who owns a keyboard, you probably have a series of different graphical figures such as (**$&%**) listed on your keyboard above a series of numbers. All you must do is ask yourself what the actual grammatical figure looks like to you and then attach that meaning to the corresponding number on the keyboard.

For instance, if you look at the symbol (**&**), is it usually located above the number 7 on a standard keyboard. So, I would remember what image corresponds to the number **07** (OG- Oscar the grouch) and then determine that the symbol (**&**) itself looks like a twisted coat hanger. Therefore, I now have an image for that symbol, as I can picture a twisted coat hanger coming out of a garbage can. I have also attached another list of the other **most common punctuation marks** in the English language as well as some related definitions that I have used in the past to help remember them. Feel free to either use this list or create your own images, just decide what the icon looks or sounds like to you. This can be useful for you when it comes to memorizing lines of poetry or a written speech.

Comma (,)- bird winds

Period (.)- large hole

Quotation ("")- a cloud above a person's head while they are thinking

Underline-(___) bed stretcher

Colon- (men's cologne being sprayed

Semi-colon- (;) toilet seat

Slash mark- (/) Tower of Pisa

Hyphen- (-)fin of a shark

Okay now, let us see if we can finally use all of these literary memory skills to test how well you can actually memorize a famous poem or speech. Included below is a time-honored favorite poem of mine that came from the great English poet **Robert Frost**. This was one of the first poems I had ever read from him during my days in high school. It is entitled "*Stopping by Woods on a Snowy Evening*". For this exercise, I would like for you to write out the exact words and punctuation marks on one sheet of paper, and then cover that paper up once you are done. Next, I would like you to take out another piece of paper and number it from 1-20, as there are 20 lines in this poem, including title, references, and name. At this point, turn back over the poem that you have just copied and try to memorize it, word for word, without writing it down on the other sheet. Give yourself at least 15 minutes to memorize the entire poem.

Make sure you time yourself with a stopwatch. Then turn over the original sheet and use your answer number sheet to write down as many of the words and punctuation marks to the best of your recollection for each individual sentence. Once you are done, go back and see if you got it perfect, or if there were some mistakes. Give yourself <u>5 points</u> for each line that you got perfect (that includes capitalization as well). Your top score should be <u>100 points</u>. Don't forget to include the title, date, reference info, and the author's name. Good luck. (to remember or not to remember, that is the question, haha)

<u>Stopping by Woods on a Snowy Evening</u>

by Robert Frost
1922 New Hampshire Volumes

Whose woods these are I think I know.
His house is in the village though;
He will not see me stopping here
To watch his woods fill up with snow.

My little horse must think it queer
To stop without a farmhouse near
Between the woods and frozen lake
The darkest evening of the year.

He gives his harness bells a shake
To ask if there is some mistake.
The only other sound's the sweep
Of easy wind and downy flake.

The woods are lovely, dark and deep,
But I have promises to keep,
And miles to go before I sleep,
And miles to go before I sleep
"to my friend Louis U"

CHAPTER 12

Book memory

When I was 15 years old and growing up in the small town of Goshen, I remember my late grandmother once buying both me and my brother a large set of the most recent volumes of the Encyclopedia Britannica, at least 24 different books in one large set. My brother and I plowed through each of these treasured books, hoping to grasp all of the different concepts, facts, and ideas that were listed throughout each glorious volume. However, as I continued to read page after page, I started to notice that I was taking less and less of an interest in what was written.

I wondered why I was feeling this way, given the enormous amount of information before me, just waiting to be devoured by my young and energetic brain. And it was then that I realized why I was feeling so depressed after reading these books: I was not able to remember one single thing that I had been reading. Even though I could easily understand what each page or article was saying about each subject, I could not for the life of me be able to recall much of what I had just read only just minutes ago. I felt as though all of this information was just going to make me feel worse, unless of course I chose to use it as a source for one of my high school papers.

Needless to say, I was sort of wondering what it would be like if I could one day be able to remember and recall all of the different subjects and topics listed within these great pamphlets at any given time. However, the more I tried to read the same pages over and over again, the less I cared about what the actual subject matter was really about. In the educational world, we refer to this as "<u>rote</u>

memorization", which I talked about earlier in the book. The process of repeating the same information over and over again does tends to help you recall the information again for a short while, but it does not help you to understand or comprehend it, as it becomes just a meaningless series of random words stuck together.

It was during this time that I was introduced to another one of my favorite childhood heroes (although fictional), who seemed to possess an "**encyclopedic knowledge**" about many different subjects and topics. It was this fictional character that would inspire me to want to learn more about how to remember information about random subjects in my head, so that if one day I wanted to recall some important fact about a specific subject at a specific time, I would have no problem in retrieving it.

During the 1890's, a series of books came out by a very famous author by the name of Sir Arthur Conan Doyle. One of his most beloved characters was as eccentric yet brilliant minded consulting detective for the Scotland Yard police department, named **Sherlock Holmes**. Throughout most of the series of books, which were written from the perspective of his able bodied and reluctant partner, Dr. John Watson, the legendary deductive genius himself traveled throughout the cities of London and other villages, solving random crimes and conspiracies that most other officers in the Scotland Yard police department were powerless to resolve.

Despite his acute sense of observation as well as his scientific methods of deductive reasoning and logic, one other area of mental capacity that seemed to describe Sherlock Holmes well enough, was his *encyclopedic knowledge* of variously different subjects that he used as reference materials. He would use such knowledge when he was trying to make sense of whatever information was presented to him at the time. Whether it was what type of dirt soil sample was staining a person's shoes, to whether or not a person was wearing a specific type of boot to conceal a hidden medical injury, Sherlock Holmes always seemed to know the hidden answer to any unrelated piece of information placed before him. However, he almost never seemed to be carrying around any books or reference materials with him when he went about his crime solving travels. So how can it be that he was able to recall all of this valuable information at any time as if it was just on the tip of his tongue?

According to Watson's description of Holmes, he claims that Sherlock had basic general knowledge, and other times extensive understanding, of the following different subjects: politics, botany, geology, chemistry, human anatomy, sensational Literature, and British law. From what we understand about the character, Holmes had spent years of his life researching all of these varied topics either through books or newspapers, and had somehow managed to store all of that information somewhere in his head, so that when the time comes for him to retrieve such information during the course of an investigation, all he has to do is just travel through his memory palace, or as he called them his "brain attic", and the information that he previously learned is located and retrieved for such purposes.

As a child reading these books, I thought that this was just something that only the gifted or intelligent could do. But as I grew older, I realized that, although this character was strictly fictionalized, most of his psychological traits and abilities were based upon real people. It was these real people and their special cognitive abilities that helped inspire Sir Arthur Conan Doyle to combine all of their different personality traits together, and eventually mold them into the genesis of the most famous fictional detective in modern literature history.

So, rather than continue to indulge my love and admiration for the man most famous for using the phrase "elementary my dear Watson", I will now begin to explore with you how you can use the memory palace techniques and link methods to create your own version of the Holmes' "brain attic". First of all, let us review some of the things that you have already learned, or hopefully are still in the process of learning so that it can be used to help you to discover your own encyclopedic knowledge. Remember earlier when we talked about how to remember birthdays? Well, that information can also be used to recall **historical dates and facts**.

All you need to do for this is to come up with some different icons or images in your head to try to categorize which dates are important and for what reasons (not every historical date is based on a birthday). Below I have created a list of **8 different types of historical dates** that most history books usually list in chronological order. Your objective is to come up with an <u>associated image or characters</u> for each category of historical date so that you can later place that image before your numbers memory images for the actual date. I have included some ideas about what images I prefer to use to differentiate all of the different types of dates. Feel free to make up whatever images or characters you can think of that can be associated with each category listed below.

<u>Birth</u>: I picture a baby wrapped in a blanket

<u>Death</u>: I picture a casket being lowered into the ground

<u>Marriage</u>: I picture a wedding cake

<u>Divorce</u>: I picture an old, torn up recliner chair (don't ask)

<u>Fight or conflict</u>: I picture a bunch of soldiers fighting

<u>Change in occupation</u>: I picture a crown being placed on someone's head

<u>Creation or change of something</u>: I picture a lab Bunsen beaker

<u>Discovery or idea</u>: I picture a lightbulb floating over someone's head

<u>Failure or loss</u>: I picture a report card with a large letter F, written in red.

Sometimes the event is so well known or famous, that you can easily remember what the event looked like and then try to link that picture to the actual date itself, using your numbers codes. So, if I wanted to remember that the Titanic sank on April 15th 1912, I could easily picture the numbers 04 (**OD**) 15 (**AE**) 19(**AN**) and 12 (**AB**) by creating the following scene: Odie the Dog (**04**) is writing on a chalk board (**15**) about the sinking of the Titanic (<u>a boat sinking</u>) as Anna Nicole Smith (**19**) is trying to scratch it off the board with a Zorro sword (**12**). This seems to be extremely silly and does not make much sense, but like I said earlier, the weirder the picture, the more likely you will be able to recall it later. However, if you wanted to remember that the Japanese bombed Pearl Harbor on December 7, 1941, you would have to come up with an image that reminds you of Pearl Harbor, such as a Japanese bomber, a battleship on fire, or some other related image that makes sense to you. And then connect this to the following numbers: 12 (AB), 07 (OG), 19 (AN) and 41 (DA). The rest is up to you; just try to make each historical event into <u>a story within itself</u>, full of <u>odd and unusual scenarios</u> to help you remember it longer and easier.

Another mnemonic skill that we have already touched upon in the previous chapters, deals with <u>vocabulary words</u>. As you might remember, the <u>substitution method</u> states that if the word does not make sense to you or if you are not sure what it means, try to think of either how the word actually sounds or looks, and then use this substituted image to help you recall the word later. For this purpose, if you were trying to remember the **definitions of random vocabulary word**, all you would have to do is first come up with <u>an image for the actual word itself</u>, and then try to make the definition almost seem like a story that is somehow connected to such word image. For example, if I wanted to remember the definition of the word "<u>**obsequious**</u>", according to Webster's Dictionary, that word actually means " **to be characterized by or showing servile complaisance or deference, such as fawning or to be sycophantic**.

Now, in order to better remember this word for future reference, one way that I could go about visualizing it is to first come up with an image for the word itself. For this particular vocabulary word, I realize that it sounds like the word sounds like "Hobbs", "seek", and "keys". So, I can easily picture the cartoon character Hobbs the cat, trying to locate a missing pair of keys. That takes care of most of the word itself, the rest will easily fall into place when I say it. As far as the definition is concerned, I realize that the word can be described as meaning that a person *is trying to be servile or like a butler*, and *trying to bow down or defer* to the authority of another person, much to their annoyance or chagrin.

With that idea in mind, I can pretty much picture Hobbs the Cat, trying to find a pair of keys, which he then picks up shakenly and shows to a butler, who is getting annoyed by the fact that such cat is jingling them in front of his face. Once I do that, I tell myself a story about what images I have actually seen and explain to myself why it is relevant to the vocabulary word itself. Now, the actual word has its own individual story and images to better help delineate its meaning.

That is pretty much all you need to do in order to completely know the vocabulary word and its related definition. The most important point to make when it comes to vocabulary word definitions, is that you must have an understanding of what the word truly "represents or implies" in terms of its definition. That way you can better comprehend why the word is so important and what the importance of the word really is. Always consult a thesaurus for words that are synonyms for your unknown vocabulary words if this helps you to get a better idea of what the actual word truly means. And if the thesaurus does not help out, try to ask either a teacher or a friend what the word genuinely represents in their own words.

Lastly, one final idea of trying to remember information from a book can be used through the practice of the link method for your 100 mnemonic characters or images, which you created earlier for your numbers memory. In this instance, try to imagine if you were to be able to remember the exact order of 100 different English words, over the course of several sentences, and could precisely remember the exact location of each and every word. All that you would have to do is come up with an image or icon to represent each individual word, and then connect it somehow to one of your 100 characters or images from before, and that is it.

So, if the 9th word in a sentence is the term "worm", I could easily recall the image for the number 09 as **ON**, or Olivia Newton John. Therefore I could picture her from the movie "Grease", in the front seat of the grease lightning car, with a large "worm" driving at the wheel. From there, you can easily recall at least 100 different words that are used in several sentences after just several minutes of coming up with substitute images for each number character.

However, if you really want to impress your teachers or your classmates (or whoever you are in contact with), how about we try to remember the **general subject** of an actual fictional story book? Well, for this particular memory system, you could probably be capable of remembering the actual course of events for at least the first 100 pages of a fiction book, simply by applying the same principles listed in the previous paragraph. However, the only hard part about this particular memory skill is that you would have to literally read all 100 pages of the book, and take some notes on the side, so that you could refer to such information at a later time. Don't worry; it is not too hard to come up with some style of taking notes that is conducive to better memorization. The method that I use to do this takes several steps. (I will give you the actual name of a note taking method later on in the chapter)

First, before I read the book, I take out a lined sheet of paper and put a number on each and every line, on both sides of the paper, and other sheets if needed. Then I read only one page at a time, I do not go onto the next page until I am confident that I have a general understanding of what the first page was about. During this time, I tell myself what actions or events just occurred on the first page, and try to summarize it according to the following equation: (**characters, actions, places, and consequences**, or **CAPC**). That means that, when I am done reading the first page of a fictional story book, I ask myself who are the main characters that were present at this time, what actions were the characters actually committing, where were these events occurring, and what if any consequences did these actions have on others around them. This is very similar to the **PAO** or **person-action-object** lesson that was talked about earlier. You can also always take out a pencil or a pen and draw columns down the length of the paper itself, and then label each column with the header for any of the CAPC terms, if this helps you to conceptualize what each sentence is really saying.

So, if I read a book about Sherlock Holmes, and on the first page it says that he is introducing himself to Watson in his study, and that Watson is upset by his manners, all I really have to do is write down the following words on the first line of the paper: Sherlock, introduce, in office, to Watson, made angry". And from there, I would picture Sherlock standing in his office, talking to and shaking the hand of

Watson, who is looking very angry at that time, and then place those images from left to right in my "brain attic". And that is all the words I will write for that one line for that one individual page, unless of course there is more information or events that are occurring on that same particular page. Most lined paper is generally not too wide and can only hold enough space for several words on it before you reach the end of the sheet. So please be selective about what words you use, and why you chose to use them, as they will serve as reference points in your memory and your mind.

Like I said, try to read each page and try to summarize it in just a few words about what is actually happening overall in general. And then use the previously mentioned <u>algorithm</u> in order to further delineate what each individual page is really all about. Also don't forget to use some of your previously mentioned historical date icons as well, as there might not be too many dates in a fiction book, but there will probably be some births, deaths, conflicts, and other related events occurring throughout. And once you are done with the whole CAPC format, just try to connect your series of images for the number 01 or OA. And then attach that story to the overall scene that you have just created using the algorithm. That way, when you are done reading the first 100 pages, you will be able to remember the actual course of events for the first 100 numbered pages simply by just using both the link method and the algorithm that I mentioned earlier.

If you need some advice on how to organize notes in order to better memorize non-fictional facts from either a textbook or a workbook, I might suggest a very specific method of note taking that is designed for memorizing large quantities of information. **The Charting Method** is a perfect method for taking notes that involves a lot of information, such as facts and statistics, which need to be learned for long term memory. The information can be organized into <u>several columns</u>, similar to a table or spreadsheet. Each column represents a <u>unique category</u> which makes the rows easily comparable. This type of note-taking method is great for college students when it comes to simply jotting down large amounts of data and other related information. Below is an example of what a charting note would look like, as well as some historical information to remember for a later date. You can chose to use as many rows or columns as you can fit on paper, as long as you are able to have enough room in one of your memory palaces to store such materials.

Date	Person	Place	Importance
April 15th, 1865	Abraham Lincoln (dead)	Ford's Theater	Hunt for J.W Booth

In this method, you would lable the top of each column with the type of information that you're going to memorize and review it from left to right. In a history class, for example, you may use the labels "Date," "Person," "Place" and "Importance." So, if you wanted to remember the day of Abraham Lincoln's death and what later happened to this country, it would look something like this: April 15th, 1865, Abraham Lincoln, Ford's Theater, and the hunt for John Wilkes Booth. Then you would place each of these different informative items into different rooms of your memory palace. For the date itself, you could picture an image for a historical date, such as a calendar, and then try to use your number's memory codes to represent the date.

For example, the date of Lincoln's death was April 15, 1865. In one room, you could come up with images of the numbers 04, 15, 18, and 65, and then just have them interacting with each other, next to an icon for a date. In another room of your palace, you could picture Abraham Lincoln himself next to a symbol implying death, and then in the next room you could picture a Ford Car inside of a theater, followed closely by another scene involving a man running away into a phone booth. And if you wanted to remember what page of the book such information is contained on, you could simply start off your memory place with an image of one of your 100 number character images. You could see this image standing to the left of the initial calendar date numbers, so that it can be your lead off image, thereby helping you to connect all the remaining facts together.

And at this point, you should have no problems trying to remember historical dates, vocabulary words and definitions, information from textbook, as well as general story lines for fictional books. Just think about how wonderful it would be if you could apply all of these same techniques and tasks towards memorizing the basic information regarding any subject of study, such as biology, chemistry, or criminal justice. You might be able to recall hundreds of needed vocabulary words at any given time, be capable of remembering the names and dates of important figures for each field of study, and be able to read exactly 100 pages of a non-fictional book about your particular subject and remember the actual order of events throughout such pages.

Though this does take some time and a lot of reading, note taking, and asking questions, don't be too worried. With enough time, practice and effort, all of the information will begin to stick in your head longer and deeper so that you can recall it again later with perfect precision. That way you won't have to simply just keep reading over the materials again and again, hoping that you will eventually get the idea. (I wish I still had those old encyclopedias at this time, would be nice to go ahead and try it again).

Anyway, feel free to go ahead and try these different techniques and methods on the following exercise material about another famous politician in US history, Franklin Delano Roosevelt. I have included relevant historical information about this person, such as his birthday, where he went to school, when/where he got married, when he took office and when/where he died. For this exercise, I will be presenting such information to you in a regular paragraph form. Your job is to read through all of the information and then transpose such data onto another sheet of paper, using any of the previously mentioned note taking lessons from this chapter.

At the end of the exercise, I have included several questions that you must answer correctly in order to pass this exercise. Get your note-taking paper ready in advance so that all you have to do is just list the important information down as you read. Write the questions down on your separate answer sheet before you start memorizing anything at this time. I don't want you to have any reason to open the book again and see the information in front of you. You will have **5 minutes** to both read through the information itself and then take memory notes in whatever style or method you would like. You will then have another **5 minutes to simply memorize** the information in the manner in which you took notes on it. Once your next 5 minutes are done, flip your page over, close the book itself, and then answer the following questions based upon your memory of the information presented. Practice this at least once a day for a week, and see how much easier it gets by the end of such week. Get ready, get set, go for it. (Extra- extra, read all about it, ha ha)

"Franklin Delano Roosevelt was born on January 30, 1882 in Hyde Park, NY. Franklin Roosevelt graduated from Harvard in 1903 with a BA in history. On March 17, 1905, Roosevelt married Eleanor in New York City. The 1932 United States presidential election was held on Tuesday, November 8, 1932. Roosevelt died in his cabin in Warm Springs, Georgia on April 12, 1945."

1. What is Franklin D. Roosevelt's birthday, and where was he born?
2. In what year did Franklin Roosevelt graduate from college and what school did he attend? What did he major in?
3. When did Franklin Roosevelt get married? Whom did he marry and where was the wedding?
4. When did Franklin Roosevelt win the US presidential election?
5. Where did Franklin Roosevelt die? What was the date of his death?

Chapter 13

How to monitor progress and prepare the journey journal

Wow, I bet you were probably wondering just how you can be able to monitor your own progress in terms of your memory training regimen. Or perhaps know what to do when you discover some of your strengths and weaknesses. As a dedicated therapist, part of my treatment in working with clients, is to ask them to use some self-reflection techniques when they go home, and to monitor how well they think they are doing in therapy by reporting back to me about their progress afterwards. This requires a lot of honesty and self-analysis, as most people just expect you to tell them what to do and how to fix their problems. Part of your ability to improve your memory will rest upon you taking the time to look back at yourself and realize not just what you are doing wrong, but also what you have been doing right. This way, you will better understand what your strengths and weaknesses are and how to capitalize on them. While there is no set or measurable way to precisely calculate any of this self-knowledge, let me tell you a little bit about my own self realizations into the powers and weaknesses of my own memory, and how I got about evaluating my own progress.

First, one of the reasons why I had given you a weekly memory test guide sheet for almost all of your activities was not just to see how well you could do for the first week or two. It was designed for you to monitor your speed and accuracy for each individual memory task. Hopefully, you have kept most of the corresponding exercises and answer sheets with you from all previous assignments. Now, the important thing to consider is how much your memory has improved, and what areas are you still struggling with.

During your initial exercise, I was trying to gather a baseline of your innate abilities for memory, some of us probably did better or worse than expected. And then, hopefully after reading through most of these different chapters, as well using my guidance and techniques, and practicing and rehearsing them over and over, you should have seen a huge improvement in your memory. Perhaps you discovered that you were able better able to remember the exact sequence of information more accurately then before. Maybe you were more capable of storing information longer into your long-term memory, and then eventually recalling it back hours or even days later. Or, maybe you were fortunate enough to discover your own particular memory system using some of the guidelines that I presented to you earlier. The point is this, how exactly did your memory improve?

Below is a list of **six questions** that I continue to ask myself each time I either show some significant improvement in my memory abilities or when I develop a new cognitive related skill on my own. Try to ask yourself these questions at least <u>once a month</u> when you have the chance to sit down and look over your previous months' scores. You can choose to use this list as <u>an internal reference guide</u> to better develop self-awareness and insight into your abilities, or you can create your own internal memory checklist for yourself, whichever option is more comfortable for you.

1: *How much faster was I able to memorize the same amount and type of information from one week or month to the next? (Seconds, minutes) Use the previous memory assignments and continue to score yourself each time.*

2: *How much more accurate was I in being able to recall the same amount and type of information from one week or month to the next? (percentage). See how close you are coming to achieving perfect recall on any activity.*

3: *What characters or images was I most comfortable with using in my memory? (keep these characters as they have been working well) Which characters am I least comfortable with using? (see if you would like to change them if needed)*

4: *What memory palaces were easiest for me to navigate through? (continue to use these for speed related exercises) Which ones are not as easy to navigate through? (consider changing or amending the locations and only use them for untimed exercises until you are more comfortable)*

5: *What field of information (numbers, words, cards, binary codes) did I find it easiest to memorize? (each one of us will find one field to be our favorite at some point). Which fields do I struggle with in terms of amount of effort or time in recalling? (try working on those fields more often to get used to them)*

6: *What if any shortcuts or other methods could I use to try to improve my recall times and scores, and how comfortable am I in using them? (think outside the box and experiment from time to time)*

The next thing to start paying attention to is something that I commonly refer to as my "**journey journal**". (try saying that five times fast, haha). By journey journal, what I really mean is that I have collected and organized together an entire binder, or journal in this regard, containing all of my written memory palaces mnemonic codes for various types of information, suggestions for how to both navigate through each palace, and how to place each different type of information. So, in this way, I have created an organizer for my organizer. On each page, I have a different memory palace, which is clearly labeled with the name of the palace itself. On that same page, I have included a diagram of the memory palace with related numbers of all of the different locations for such palace, as well as a written list of the different locations and their associated descriptions.

I have categorized all of my memory palaces into different units, such as palaces for my mother's side of the family (grandparents, aunt and uncles' houses), my father's side of the family (cousins, nieces and nephews' houses), my wife's side of the family (in-laws and other associated relatives), and work place related palaces (current office, former offices and houses of some colleagues). Below is an example of one page of my journey journal, try to see how I have it organized so that you get a better idea about how to create one yourself.

(#1) FIRST FLOOR OF MY HOUSE IN MIDDLETOWN (10 locations)

Location #	Description of location (include what the location actually is and what it means)
First location	Door (items #1-4)
2nd	TV set (items #5-8)
3rd	Couch (items #9-12)
4th	Coffee table (items #13-16)
5th	Easy chair (items #17-20)
6th	China set cabinet (items #21-24)
7th	window (items #25-28)
8th	Lamp (items #29-32)
9th	Piano stand (items #33-36)
10th	Door out (items #36-40)

In all, I have about *40 different memory palaces*, which I can use at any given time I want. You don't have to categorize your palaces exactly as I have done, however it does help to have some type of organization for such information, as it makes it easier to recall the codes and palaces easier when you are out in the field and trying to remember information on the spot as opposed to being at home. As far as my mnemonic codes are concerned, I have put those codes in the back of my journey journal, with a title for each list of information and the associated images or codes for each piece of information. I have lists for all of my number codes, card codes, prefix word codes, personal information codes, common name codes, binary number codes, and other related topics that I have thought about throughout the years. There is no limit as to how much information you can decode, categorize, chunk or organize, as long as there is a way where you can later input such information into one of your memory palaces. The choice is up to you as to what you want to remember the most, and how you can transform that information into something that you cannot forget.

The third and final thing to consider is to make sure that you give yourself at least a few minutes a day, or perhaps an hour a week, where you can dedicate yourself to reviewing some of your memory palaces, and related memory codes. Please try to test yourself on any one of the five previously mentioned memory tasks (numbers, binary codes, words, cards, personal information) on any given day of the week. You can try to work on the same field of memory for the same corresponding day of the week if you like, this also makes it easier to determine how well you are doing in your memory training regimen, as it will remind you if you have forgotten or skipped a day of training during the week. I usually work on card memory on Mondays and word memory on Tuesdays.

The schedule you put together is entirely your decision. Just try to make sure that you have enough time each day to go over what memory palaces you want to use for that day, as well as the related codes of information for the individual memory subject you plan to work on. I spend at least 10 minutes each day going over my number codes and 5 minutes going over at least 3 memory palaces, before I even attempt to do any exercises for memory on any day. How much time you spend on rehearsing and planning depends on your comfort level with your palaces and related information codes. Try to come up with some type of training schedule that works with your current work and family life schedule, set aside some time each day of a week for a different type of activity or exercise.

As a Boy Scout, one of the most important lessons that I learned, aside from survival and leadership skills, was the all-important phrase that all Boy Scouts swear by: <u>Be Prepared</u>. It could not be any simpler than that. Each time you rehearse your character codes by mentally picturing them in your head, or walking through your memory palaces while using the "as I walk over here" routine, you are preparing yourself for any future memory challenge. Most of us will sometimes assume that after doing this hundreds of times, that there is real need to continue practicing or rehearing each time we try it again. Well, that would make sense if we were actually going over something that we already know from our childhood, like the alphabet or our basic numbers. However, in this case, what you are really doing is trying to "relearn" the alphabet and your numbers.

Since this goes against everything that we have ever been taught, you will most likely have to go back and review your codes and palaces each time you set upon the task of trying to memorize something again. I know that it feels like a lot of extra work and stress, but believe me; you will see the results very fast. Even though I have been on numerous camp outs throughout my time in Boy Scouting, each time I was getting ready for another excursion, I would always have to go back to the same "Kim Games" drills for myself by remembering personal possessions I would need before I left the house. So, take it from me (the Eagle Scout that I am), when it comes to getting ready for any type of memory challenge, before you do anything else, always be prepared.

By incorporating these three methods of self-monitoring on a monthly basis, and reading through your journey journal from time to time, you will have a much better capacity for being ready and prepared for almost any type of memory challenge that comes your way in the future. Don't be afraid to try to keep some of your old scores with you for reference purposes. (you don't need to keep them all, lets try to save paper here) And occasionally look through your journey journal when you want to refresh your memory in terms of your various memory journeys and related informational codes. You can't expect to remember and recall all of the information in your "journals" at any given time, however the more you practice and rehearse the information, the more you will have memorized your memory language in of itself (talk about a double positive, huh?)

CHAPTER 14

Self-help/self-care tips, and long term memory

Like any good therapist, part of my job is to teach my clients certain skills and techniques related to how to handle life stressors through strategies such as coping mechanisms, understanding of mental defense structures, and other therapeutic related materials. For this chapter, I will be having you sit down on the couch (not literally) and go over any concerns that you might have in regard to working on improving your memory. I realize that most of us will experience some type of euphoria after learning this particular type of memory change-over in many different ways, but I wanted to go over some of the issues that I have learned myself from experience that have helped me to overcome some obstacles and boundaries in my own personal pursuit of memory excellence.

First and foremost, let's stop talking about your brain and memory, and start talking about you as an individual person, and what are some of the things that you might be going through in life. There are many different variables that can affect your ability to <u>work on or improve your memory</u>. The three most common factors that have impacted my cognitive abilities during the day are <u>stress, food and sleep</u>. For myself, I have always noticed that if I am very busy or harried during the day, I tended to feel that I didn't have enough time to work on my memory, and simply just told myself that I would get to it at a later date. At first, this was not so much a problem. But then, I started to get into the habit of putting off my memory exercises for a week or two weeks at a time, and then one time a entire month. It was then that I started to realize that the brain is like any other muscle in the body. If you don't use it, you start to lose it. That is an old expression that my teachers used to tell me in high school, and it still rings true to this day.

In order to avoid losing this precious muscle due to procrastination, please try to find at least 15-20 minutes a day, when you are not being overloaded with work or family, in order to either rehearse your memory codes, go through your memory palaces briefly, or just try another memory exercise to see how well you do. Each morning I mentally go through all my numbers and card related memory codes, so that I can keep them fresh in my head, and it only takes a few minutes. Just by trying to make a little time for yourself each day (if possible, don't wait for more than a week), you are basically keeping the wheels in your brain strong and moving along, and like any good athlete, you are doing your basic daily "warm-up" so that your brain stays in top shape.

However, before you start to believe that this is all you need to look out for, I should warn you that just being overwhelmed or busy during the day is not the only thing that could affect or slow down your memory during your future rehearsals. I have also noticed that, after I eat a large meal, I tend to get very tired and lethargic for at least the next hour or two. While I am not suggesting you starve yourself in order to improve your memory, be advised that when most of us consume a large amount of food, our bodies begin to slow down, and our minds tend to do just the same. I cannot concentrate or focus as well as I would like after a large meal.

So, the best thing to do is to make sure you give yourself some time in between meals to digest so that you cannot too tired or full to recall the information when you need to. Sometimes it is a good idea to try to eat certain amounts of food before you undertake any memory challenge, as well as different types of food that are guaranteed to help promote mental clarity. Food such as blueberries, protein snacks, caffeine related teas and coffees, as well as perhaps oatmeal or peanuts, will all supply you with the appropriate nutrients and minerals needed to continue to keep your brain strong and healthy.

Also, the amount of sleep that you get each night is very detrimental to your abilities to use your memory the following day. When I am sleep deprived or exhausted the next day, I know that I will have to work twice as hard, or drink twice as much coffee, in order to keep up the demands of my day, let alone my future memory challenges. So, as long you as can make sure that you get a good night sleep the day before your memory challenge, your brain will be better prepared and ready for your next memory assignment. Sometimes it is a good idea to try to take a nap or get some rest before you try to accomplish a memory task.

It has been shown that by simply closing your eyes and trying to mentally tune out everything around you for at least 2 minutes before you start a memory challenge, you can easily increase your speed and your performance abilities. In addition, trying things like meditation, deep breathing and guided imagery before you go to sleep at night can help to improve the quality of your sleep before you shut your eyes, therefore giving you a better REM cycle so that you wake up refreshed the next morning. You will definitely feel a change in your energy level and motivation the following day after you try to slow down or tune down your brain before you go to sleep.

Secondly, if you have already created your own "journey journal", try to look through it entirely at least once a week, briefly skimming through the pages and asking yourself if there is anything in there that you are not completely sure of or comfortable with. By staying abreast of the information that you have compiled in regard to your palaces and other related information, you will better remember it easier. So that when the time does come for you to test your memory out either in private or in the real world, you won't have to try to locate your journal and flip through all the pages to find the information that you are looking for. Occasionally, I do make a change to another memory palace in my journal so that it feels more normal and easier for me to travel through it. You will also start to notice that certain palaces don't always feel convenient the way that you have arranged them, please feel free to change some of the focal points or locations that you have used before in order to make it easier to navigate through such palaces. Make any needed corrections in your journal so that you have all your information up to date.

Third, before you are ready to start on a particular memory challenge, try to block out everything else in the world around you by closing your eyes and taking a few deep breaths without anyone interrupting you. Do this for usually about 2-3 minutes at a time if possible. Usually it is a good idea during these quiet moments, to remind yourself, not just about your past mistakes or errors in memory, but about your past accomplishments and achievements in memory. Each time I feel nervous or afraid to take on another memory challenge, I silently calm myself down and remind myself of how far I have come in the past few years and that I have already made significant improvements in my mental abilities that I did not have years ago. This makes me feel more confident and motivated with regards to any future memory task. And from there on, I am ready to take on whatever memory challenge lies ahead of me.

Eventually, this process makes me feel calm and relaxed in my abilities and strengths. The point to remember is to not get too cocky or arrogant in your thinking. Don't always assume that you cannot fail on your next memory task, remember no one is perfect. Try to keep yourself in check at times and remember that you are better than when you first got started, but that you can still have mistakes unless you truly focus and concentrate hard. There have been times when I was very disappointed with my results during certain memory tasks as I had made lots of huge mistakes, wondering how I could have done so terrible at them.

However, afterwards I reminded myself that only I myself can make mistakes, as the techniques themselves are always guaranteed to work. This lets me know that the mistake is not with the memory techniques themselves, but only with me as the user. And that I must learn what I had done wrong earlier in order to correct it the next time I try another memory task. You don't have to worry too much about it, as mistakes will sometimes happen. What is important to remember is to try to learn from your mistakes as opposed to punishing yourself for them. That is why I suggest you try to focus on your accomplishments in memory tasks and to feel good about yourself for the lessons you have learned through trial and error. This helps you to feel more self-assured in your abilities, and to realize what you have left to work on.

But remember, no one in memory sports is perfect, so always try to keep yourself in check.

Fourth, when you are actively trying to remember information by placing it in your memory palaces, it is important to develop a certain speed or rhythm that feels comfortable for you. I assure you that, when Lance Armstrong first learned to ride a bike as a child, he was not going quite as fast as he was later in life during the Tour de France. The old adage of "you must learn to crawl before you walk, and walk before you run", is very important in this endeavor. At first, you will most likely start out at a slow and steady speed when you begin to use the memory palace or link methods. You will notice that one piece of information takes several seconds to put into place before you are ready for the next bit of information to memorize.

That is why I suggested to you earlier that you time yourself on your various assignments. This will let you know what you baseline speed for memory is, and to see how well you can input information into your brain within a certain time. Try to be honest with yourself; don't go too fast too soon. You will inevitably speed up as your become more comfortable with your memory codes and palaces. By going too fast, most memory athletes tend to miss some information or skip a location in their palaces, which causes the person to make lots of mistakes during recall.

One way to learn how to pace yourself is to either go out and purchase a metronome (which is used in musical performance in order to count the beats), or just simply use the old school methods that my mother taught me (such as repeating "one-one thousand", or "one-Mississippi"). By timing yourself or tapping your foot on the ground for a few seconds to this beat, you can determine at what speed you would like to proceed with in memorizing your information. I used to be able to memorize information at the same speed it took me to repeat the "One-Mississippi expression", as it this takes longer to say this. Now, I am at the speed where I can input data in my memory palaces at the rate of time that it takes me to repeat the phrase "One- One-thousand", as this is slightly quicker to say. The most important thing to determine is to figure out what pace you are most comfortable with when creating images and traveling through your memory palaces. Try to stick to that pace for now until you feel ready to start moving onto faster and quicker speeds.

Lastly, one final piece of self-help advice that I can give to you, is to try to use the reference guides that I listed earlier which helped remind you of how much information you can place in each room or location in your memory palaces. It is always a good idea to put the same amount or quantity of information in each room or location of your memory palaces so that you know the exact location of any piece of information that you are looking for. (remember the chart I used earlier about putting items #1-4 at the first location, items #5-8 at the next location, etc) This also helps you to be prepared for how much information you will be able to stuff into your particular memory palaces in the first place. Nothing frightens me more at work than to see a file drawer over stuffed with so much paper or materials so that it looks as though it will literally overflow.

Remember, your memory palaces are like organizers or files, but even those materials have limits to how much information can be placed in there. The more palaces and locations you have, the more information you can actually store for later retrieval. Just try to figure out how much information can go into each separate room and location, and overall how much data can be stored in the entire memory palace itself. Like I said earlier, I have about 40 memory palaces with at least 20-25 locations or points per palace, meaning that I have roughly 1000 different separate focal spots to use in my palaces. This lets me know how much information overall I can store into all of my palaces at any given time.

Aside from giving you some self-help advice, I would also like to give you some suggestions, so that you can understand the fundamentals of the memory technique a little bit better. For those of you who are just starting out with using the memory palace technique, let me tell you some things that I learned early in life that have helped me to have a better understanding of how to use such technique accurately. Before, when we first talked about the setting the scene technique, I described a scene of a person on the left side of a stage, having some type of interaction with someone else on the right side of the stage. As you know, this will be something that you can create in your minds, by using your inner senses and trying to picture one character on the left and another object to the right.

When I was a child, my mother used to walk around the house with me and my brother, and we played a game similar to "I Spy with my little eye". She used to take us around the house and point at various important objects in the household, and then say "**as I walk over here, I see before me, "this" and "that" looking back at me**". She did this as a way to help me and my brother remain oriented to the layout of our house. She was literally taking me on a trip through one of my very first memory palaces.

And that is why, when you first go about walking through your own house, someone else's house, or perhaps when just trying to remember a place that you saw years ago, as you are going through each room or location (physically and mentally), try to repeat this phrase to yourself out loud. While you are repeating this phrase, stop at each focal point or location you come to, and then gesture physically or mentally with your left hand extended, as you fill in the blank for the word "this", and then extend your right as you fill in the word for "that". This will help you to recall which objects you want to remember first and which ones you want to remember second.

Try to fill in these blanks for the expression, remember don't use the actual words "this" and "that" for the sentence. Instead, fill in the blanks with the characters or images' names, and then state out loud what the two characters are doing to each other. For example, if I am trying to remember the numbers 2763, I imagine the characters at a certain point in my memory palace, and I literally say to myself "as I walk over here, I see before me, Bill Gates with Christmas gifts, looking back at me". This helps to create a tiny little story for each location, as if you were walking through a fun house and just noticing all of the weird and unusual things happening around you. You will probably feel a variety of feelings and emotions at each location; this is good because it will help you to recall the information more accurately when you have done with your memorization task.

One final thought about how to improve your memory, is a lesson that can be learned in how to enhance not only your short-term memory, but also your **long-term memory** as well. In order to guarantee that the information you are about to memorize will remain in your mind for hours, days, or in possibly weeks to come, here are some basic strategies you can use to make sure that you can hold onto information even longer than you thought possible.

First, after you have memorized an entire sequence of data, try to review the information in your memory palace both forwards and backwards. Repeat this process about 3 times in a row, so that you have looked at the information in both directions at least three times. After that, try to mentally test yourself on remembering every "other" piece of information in your palace, such as the 1st, 3rd, and 5th unit of information, as well as the 2nd, 4th, and 6th unit of information (odds and evens). This way you can surprise yourself by being able to recall every other digit or unit of information without having to go straight through the entire list all over again. Now try doing this again 3 times for all groups of information, this time going both forwards and backwards for each palace.

After this step is over, stop trying to memorize the information for at least one hour or two and don't try to memorize anything else at that time. Then, after an hour or two, mentally review your memory palace just once more, both forwards and backwards to see how well you can recall the information after an hour or so of absence. Later, do the same rehearsal activities again before you go to bed that night. This should prove that you are able to remember information even hours later. Now, try to rehearse it again briefly the following morning, and see if the information is still fresh in your mind.

At this point, the images and characters should be so clear and memorable that you will have absolutely no problems recalling them again later the next night. Just make sure that you don't use that same memory palace again for any other new information, as this will cause you to go through the chalkboard effect, where you might confuse some information with older data. Try to reserve this memory palace for no other purpose than this one memory project. As you can probably guess, this is very similar to rote memorization, whereby you go over the same information over and over, only this time you have already learned a new technique in order to better recall the information in a different way.

CHAPTER 15

Practical uses (groceries, instructions, chores, apts, bills)

I know that most of us who have already gone through reading all of the previous chapters and are probably wondering one very important question that has not been answered: <u>when will I ever truly be able to use this in my domestic life</u>? Well, you would be surprised to know that I have come up with at least <u>5 different ways</u> that you can use some of your memory skills to help out in various different arenas of your household life. Even though it is possible to use many of the previously learned lessons to your advantage in just about any facet of your life, many of you are still wondering about just how to simplify such methods in order to make them easier to use for more common activities that go on in your households. As there are just so many different topics to cover at this time, I will only address five main topics of practical usage: **groceries, instructions, chores, appointments, and bills.** (I consider my wife Erin to be a domestic genius, who already seems to know how to keep up with all of these activities with near perfect precision).

First, let's go over some other household or domestic related topics that you have already learned to memorize. For example, if you wanted to remember the phone number or the birthday of a friend or relative, such memory lesson was already introduced earlier in the chapter on personal data. If you wanted to recall the birthdays or addresses of your closest living relatives without having to check your date book or your phone again, just simply use the previous lesson on how to remember personal data, and try to use that person's house or office as a memory palace for such information. For example, if you wanted to remember when your uncle's birthday was and what his phone number is, simply try to visualize such person's house and use some of the rooms or focal points as anchors for the numbers regarding his phone number and birthday.

The same thing can be said for remembering the order and organization of a person's family tree, as long as you have the ability to either see such a diagram or have someone simply write down all the information for you on paper. This will give you an advantage at either a party or a family get together, as you will be able to know who is related to who, and you can use the names and faces memory exercise to remember their names at a later date.

So for now, the next topic to go over would be the idea of using memory techniques to recall grocery lists, instructions for tools, chores at home, appointments in the community and paying your bills (again, I defer to my wife to handle most of these activities at home, as I am domestically challenged to say the least). Anyway, I think it goes without saying that, no matter whom you are or what you do for a living, you will always have to deal with these five different topics on a regular basis. From time to time, our work lives and personal lives get so overwhelming and tiresome, that we tend to forget to pay our bills, do your chores, get the right groceries, or make it to our doctors on time.

And there are many more of us who have used a calendar or an app on our cell phones to remind us when to do such domestic things in our lives. While it is advantageous to have such technology available, or to decorate our wall calendars with random words, names, and numbers, there are more subtle and effective ways to remember all of this relevant information without having to write down everything. Here is how I have learned to use my memory skills to help me out in such personal and private arenas.

For starters, when it comes to **grocery shopping**, this is by far the easiest chore for someone to recall using the memory skills I have mentioned, yet it often becomes the most common hardship for most working professionals each week, as they struggle to come up with a lists of food materials needed for the house as well as how much money to spend. For many of us, going to the grocery store is a constant irritation that often involves looking over our list of needed foods for the week, going through each aisle, and crossing off each item until there are none left. This usually involves walking back and forth throughout the aisles, hoping not to forget certain items as we continually look at our watches, realizing how much time has already gone by. However, when you think about it like this, the store itself is pretty much organized for you in a way that can better suit you in terms of using your memory skills as long as you apply certain principles to it.

First of all, think about the fact that each <u>aisle</u> in the grocery store has a <u>number</u> already listed on it. Usually, the numbers go from 1 to possibly 12 or 14, depending on the size of the store. When you have a chance and are not in too much of a rush, go to the store just for the fun of it, and pay attention to the actual foods that are listed in each aisle, and try to notice what are the <u>three most common foods</u> for each of the numbered rows, and write this information down on a piece of paper. (keep this with you if needed)

Remember the previous lesson regarding personal information, where you were introduced to the idea of remembering what a person's favorite foods are. Well, this is the same thing. Only this time, try to picture the figure or image that you created for each numbered aisle 01-12, and place that character in your memory alongside the various foods that are associated with each aisle. For example, the first aisle in our grocery store is for foods and vegetables. My code image for 01 is an Eagle Scout. So, I picture an Eagle Scout trying to roast fruits and vegetables over a campfire (not a healthy idea, but still a great image to hold onto), and this helps me to recall what aisle to look in if I am interested in purchasing such goods.

The best part about this method is that most grocery stores do not usually change what foods are usually located in each aisle very frequently, so you will have lots of time to get used to the images and the associated foods for each character. This will give you a better chance to look over your grocery list and instead of just listing all the foods down as needed for the week, just try to organize the foods into what aisles you would most likely to be able to find them, according to your initial data sheet. If you already know that you need fruits and vegetables, try to remember what aisle always contains such foods, and usually what character is associated with that particular aisle.

Then just put the corresponding number above it in your mind. This makes going to the grocery store seem like following a map in your head, and this time you are already being told where all the necessary items are located. You will discover that you are able to get done with such shopping a whole lot faster and easier than before and this will allow you to have more time during the day to take care of any other related activities in the community. I have included a simple chart underneath to show you a mock grocery list and how to use it for memorization purposes. Try it out yourself and see what happens.

1	2	3	4	5	6	7	8	9	10
Fruits	Cereal	Milk	Paper	Beer	Soap	Meds	First aid	Meat	Pizza
Vegs	Oatmeal	Juice	Pens	Soda	Razors	Vitamins	Tissues	Cheese	Burgers
Bread	Granola	Drinks	Pencils	Water	Floss	Herbs	Pads	Dairy	Hot dog

Another personal activity that can be easily memorized is one that we often struggle with in our own lives. And that activity is the unfortunate need to have to <u>follow instructions or recipes</u> at home, whether it be trying to a complete a DIY project (do it yourself) at home, or just attempting to bake that delicious batch of cookies the same way that grandma used to make. Either way, sometimes reading instructions or recipes can be quite tiresome, stressful, or occasionally boring at times. One way to utilize your memory skills in order to make such lengthy tasks easier is to combine both numbers memory with <u>vocabulary words and action words</u> memory tasks. For instance, if you have bought a brand new device for your DIY house project, try to take out some paper and write out the steps in much simpler terms or definitions, so that it can be summarized in a way that makes more sense to you.

Consider using other certain algorithms such as <u>tool, part needed, action, desired outcome (**TPNADO**)</u>. Then try to remember what each tool or part either looks like or sounds like (hopefully you will already own enough tools in your own household so that you are already familiar with all of them). Then just link an image for the number **01** to match the algorithm for the first step, and place this in the <u>first room</u> of your memory palace. So, if the first direction requires you to take a screwdriver to screw in the bolts to the main assembly, simply just picture an image for the number 01 (an Eagle Scout for me), using a screwdriver to make a hole into a bunch of tree nuts, and that tree is being held up by a bunch of assembly parts. This lets you easily recall what is the first, second, and third <u>set of directions </u>from a manual, so that later when you go back and try to do it yourself, you won't accidentally skip a step or start from the wrong point. Like I said, try to <u>summarize</u> the directions first into a much easier to understand language, and then proceed to use both numbers and vocabulary words memory skills. Below is an example that can be used for future purposes.

Step #1	Step #2	Step #3	Step #4
Take screwdriver	Turn screw into bolts	Connect to assembly	Check over work
(image of screwdriver)	(image of screws/bolts)	(image for assembly)	(image for inspection)

The same thing can be said for <u>following a recipe book</u>, which is generally a very useful tool to use when you are cooking something new. However, if you ever misplace or lose such an item, there is a way to make sure that you never forget how to make that perfect dish of yummy food. When you have a chance, look through your favorite cook books or recipe manuals. Try to write down the favorite dishes that you most like to make. Number each recipe, with a number next to the title of each dish. Make sure that you "rename" the dishes to include words that will remind you of the dish itself, especially if the titles are too large or hard to pronounce. This will be placed into your first memory palace, along with the image for the associated number.

Then, in the next room of the memory palace, you would create images for all the actual ingredients or tools that you will need. You can either use the real name of the ingredient or tool, or a substitute word that reminds you of the items. And finally in the following rooms, you could create images for the numbered steps that follow (**1, 2, 3, 4, etc**), and then use the same formula for the <u>following instructions algorithm</u>. This is similar to the PAO method listed earlier (person, action and object).

So, if you are making scrambled eggs, first picture images for the words "scrambled" and "eggs" in the first room of your memory palace. Then, in the next room of your palace, picture the ingredients that are needed, such as eggs, pepper, salt, and possibly bacon bits. And if the first step of making that particular dish involves breaking two eggs and mixing in some of the other ingredients, you could picture the image for the number 01 (Boy Scout) again, cracking two eggs and then mixing the associated images or words for any other related ingredients into a bowl.

And then from there, you will almost never forget the steps that go into cooking or following recipes. It will take time to rewrite some of the recipes and come up with necessary vocabulary words. But if you can condense the information down or simplify it in any such way, it will make the memorization process so much easier. Plus, if you remember what this food should taste or smell like, try to incorporate such information into your memory list. Below is a simple chart for your convenience.

(#1) <u>Scrambled eggs with bacon (image of title in first memory room)</u>

eggs	Bacon	Pepper	Salt	pan	Second Room (picture each ingredient)
First crack eggs	Then add bacon	Then add pepper	Then add salt	Stir in hot pan	Third room (use associated images)
(image of eggs cracking)	(image of bacon bits)	(image of using grinder)	(image of sprinkling salt)	(image of stirring in pan)	Associated images

The next domestic item after this to talk about would be doing **weekly chores**. I know that most of us are adults and we obviously are not children anymore, however despite our maturity and years of experience in the adult world, we still have no choice but to take care of various chores around the household, unless you can afford a maid. You can easily apply a very specific memory method if you would like to allocate <u>one day a week to the completion of a specific chore</u>, as there are usually several chores to do in a week. As you remember earlier from the chapter involving personal information, I talked to you about how to remember each of the <u>seven days of the week</u> by creating various images for each day based upon either substitute names or numbers.

In this case, I usually reserve Sunday for taking out the trash, therefore I could remember my image for a large sun, and use either image by linking it to a large garbage can being dumped on the ground. Mondays are specifically scheduled for sweeping and dusting, so I could either picture the image for large wads of money being swept from the floor with a broom. As long as you are able to allocate one chore for a certain day of the week, once you get into a routine and continue to do the same activities for weeks on end, you should be able to easily recall which chore you will have to do for each day simply by reminding yourself of what day it is when you wake up in the morning. Below is a simple list that I have created myself in order to help me recall what chores are to be done during the week.

Sunday	Monday	Tuesday	Wednesday	Thursday	Friday	Saturday
garbage	sweeping	dusting	laundry	Front lawn	recycling	Gas for car
(images)	(images)	(images)	(images)	(images)	(images)	(images)

Another personal item that can be completed easily with the help of mnemonic techniques is <u>paying your bills on time</u>. There are a lot of us who are now starting to pay our bills by using our I-phones or our personal computers, and simply making electronic payments that are easily processed in a matter of seconds. However, there are other people out there who are still using personal checks to pay off each bill when it comes in the mail. At home, I have a list on my refrigerator with the names of my usual bills that I have to pay each month, such as gas/ electric, car, house, insurance, and medical. Some of you might have more or less categories of bills to pay, but regardless of your expenses, try using this memory strategy when you feel like it. Perhaps one day, I too might consider paying all of my bills electronically, but I am still a man of the 1990's who believes in using the postal service.

Each time you get a bill in the mail, try to write down what date the bill is actually due and how much money is needed. Then come up with an image for each of the several types of most common bills you regularly have to pay. When I think about my gas/electric bill, I easily think of a lot of lightbulbs scattered on the floor. Therefore, when if I get my gas/electricity bill in the mail, and it is due possibly by the 30th of the March for possibly $250, I can easily picture my images for the numbers 03, 30, a light bulb, and 250. This results in me thinking about a motorcycle (**03**) driving itself over a correctional officer (**30**), who falls down on a lot of lightbulbs (**gas/electric image**) that are scattered near a live beehive (**25**), with a ring around it (**0**). (sounds like a gruesome site, but it definitely scares me enough to remind me to pay that bill on time or else)

Finally, there comes the biggest challenge of them all, the dreaded task of trying to remember appointments that you have in the community. Nothing drives us more insane than trying to remember where we have to go either before or after work as well as trying to balance out our work lives and home lives around such hectic arrangements. However, even though we can still probably use the occasional calendars at home or possibly in put such information on our cell phones, as you probably already guessed it, there is yet still another way to apply our memory techniques for this endlessly daunting task of keeping track of appointments. For me, I usually have at least several different types of appointments that I have to attend to on a regular basis throughout the month. They usually are categorized as being related to work, doctors, legal issues, bank finances, family matters, or my car. And each category was its own individual code or symbol attached to it so that I can remember such appointment better.

In this instance, you will only have to use numbers memory codes, job titles, and substitute word images for this task. When going over your regularly scheduled appointments for the month, please try to write down such information on a sheet of paper. When I have to remember that I have an appointment to get my car worked on this Saturday around 1pm, I will simply try to picture my car driving towards an image that I have created for Saturday, or perhaps another substitute word for such day. For example, if I did have an appointment for my car on Saturday at 3pm, I would then picture my car driving near a large couch, where I am **sitting on such couch being lazy** (Saturdays in my house are usually very relaxing), while Albert Einstein is standing nearby (**15:00, or 3pm**), all while a mechanic (**job of the person that I am supposed to see**) is talking to him.

This allows me to remember that it is important for me to get to this appointment on time as it would probably end up preventing Einstein from talking to the mechanic about his thoughts on physics and relativity (**E=mc2**). So, try this out whenever you have a chance to look over your calendar for each month and see what appointments you can lock into your mind, so that when the day finally comes for you to get in your car and drive to your next appointment, you are already prepared to do so as you have already been thinking about it for some time already. Below is a chart example of several appointments that I will have to make throughout the course of one week, and how I go about remembering them.

Sunday	Monday	Tuesday	Wednesday	Thursday	Friday	Saturday
library	bank	doctor	Vets office	Store	mom	car
Images of books in the sun	Image of alarm clock going off in bank	Images of doctor with blue 222's	Image of vet wearing wedding dress	Image of Thor outside a store	Image of pizza on my mother's head	Image of couch with car driving past

CHAPTER 16

Memory demonstrations and acts to perform for others

By this time, I get you are getting pretty excited and enthusiastic about your new and profound memory skills. At this point in my own training, I started to think about how I could possibly demonstrate or perform my enhanced memory skills for others, just to show off to them about what I could do with my mind. Most of us are content with just being able to use such new abilities in our own vocational or personal lives, and that might be all that we truly want in life. However, sometimes, when you are really feeling good about yourself, it does not hurt to ask somebody to quiz you on something memory related and to let them see just how magnificent and outstanding your memory truly is. That is why I am dedicating this next chapter to the fun side of memory improvement, something that I still occasionally do for either friends or family, whenever I have a chance. And this chapter is about <u>different memory performances or demonstrations</u> that you can do in front of a live audience. (I have about **15 different memory acts** that I have made up for any occasion)

Before I start to give away some of my showcase ideas (I regularly perform these stunts around people when I am asked to), there are a few things that you will need to have with you before you do anything else. First, you will need at <u>least 4 separate decks of playing cards,</u> without any of the jokers or rule list cards included. Second, you will need something large to write on so that other people can see it, preferably a <u>chalk board, a smart board, a large poster paper,</u> of just a sheet of paper on a table, as well as a marker or a pen. You might also need to have a <u>stopwatch</u>, in case you want someone to time your memory demonstrations. You will also need to find <u>a room or space</u> where there are minimal distractions around you, as you don't want a phone going off or someone talking to you during your performances (I usually try to find a room with few windows around, and ask people to turn off their phones for a few minutes). Lastly, you could also bring <u>a book</u> with you that you will have previously read and memorized if you would like to include that as part of the act.

Okay, so now here comes the real fun part of the book. This is the part where I tell you about all of the different memory acts or performances that I have done in the past, which have been met with lots of cheers, applauses and shocked looks from others. The important point to remember before you do any of these performances is to make sure that you are prepared enough in advance for each demonstration, by going over all your codes and palaces, as well as trying to remain calm and relaxed during each performance. Be sure not to brag too much about yourself or your abilities beforehand, you don't want to offend or depress anyone in the audience who wishes they could do what you do. Make sure that you humble yourself and let others know that this is not some innate or genetic skill that you have, and that it is something that can be learned by anyone who is interested. If someone from the audience is interested in learning how you have attained such abilities, explain to them after the show about the memory palace technique, the link method or the substitution principle. Let them know that with time and practice, they too can be capable of doing what you are doing. Now then, with that in mind, let me give you a "back-stage pass" to all of my individual memory acts. (curtain call, stage left)

As for myself, I usually like to start off my memory performances with the act of <u>memorizing cards,</u> as most people usually associate this ability to someone with a keen sense of competitive card playing. My first act usually involves just with one deck of cards, where I will ask a volunteer from the audience to come up and shuffle the deck for me a few times to make sure that I am not doing it myself. After that person is done, I will then tell the audience that I am going <u>to memorize</u>

the whole deck within a certain amount of time, (usually about 2-3 minutes) and then I will ask someone in the audience to time me. Then I go ahead and memorize the entire deck in front of them, and then proceed to turn the cards over individually so that they are all facing down when finished. I will need to make sure that the first card that I memorized is on top of the pile.

Finally, I will ask the volunteer to lift up each card starting from the top of the covered deck, and I will close my eyes and recall back each card from start to finish. The person standing next to me will make sure that they hold up each card for the audience to see clearly, and then place such card on the table face up one at a time. Once the recall is done, I will then ask the volunteer to remain on stage where I will then do the recall again in reverse, having them lift up the last card first and proceeding as needed. Finally, I will take the deck from that volunteer, and then ask the audience to quiz me on any specific card in the deck, such as asking me the name of the 10th, 25th, or the 45th card. At this point I will then thumb through the deck, counting out loud, and recall the card correctly by showing it to the people. This is usually a good starting act to showcase your memory abilities as lots of people will be astounded by your abilities and ask you questions about things such as poker and blackjack.

A second act that I like to do is very similar to the first act for cards. In this one, I will ask the audience to sit down in either a row or a semi-circle around me so that I can see them all (this usually works better if you have at least 5 or more people, as smaller audiences can be overwhelmed by this). Next, I do the same trick as I did before for the first stunt, where I will have a volunteer shuffle the cards, hand the deck to me, and I will memorize them all while being timed. I will then make sure to turn the deck over as I did before and keep the first card on the top of the deck. At this point, I usually count out how many people are in the audience. I then hand out a certain number of cards to each person, making sure that I give them out in the same order as the pile was assembled. Try to make sure that the first card you give to each person is on the top of the pile that they get individually. If you have 4 people, for example, give each one 13 cards so that they all get the same amount. The first card you give each person should be on the top of their own individual pile.

Finally, look at each person and <u>call out the names of the cards that each one of them is holding</u>. This usually works well if you remember the lesson I gave you earlier about trying to decide <u>how much information to place at each location</u>. Then, by just doing the math with regards to the number of people that are there, you will already know the exact cards that each person has from the order of the deck you memorized. If you really want to impress them, don't go exactly in order for each person. Chose different people to call on and point to them and recall the cards that they each have, such as calling on the last person first and then going to the middle person next. This will truly shock the audience, as they will now know that you are probably not allowed in any casinos anymore in the area for such skills.

A third act that can be done with cards involves using <u>two decks of cards for memorization</u>. In this stunt, you will ask another volunteer to shuffle one deck of cards a few times, while you ask another volunteer to re-organize a second deck of cards so that the second deck is in perfect chronological order for all suits (Ace-King). This will be your <u>base deck</u>, you will not need to memorize this as it is entirely too easy. Then, you will go ahead and memorize an entire deck of cards while being timed, and then place that deck face down in front of you. Ask the audience to form a half circle around you so that everyone can be closer and see what is happening. You will then tell the audience that you are going to <u>re-arrange the second deck to match the order of the original first deck</u> that you memorized in under 5 minutes (this is why it is a good idea for the second deck to be in perfect order, as you will know where all the needed cards are).

At this point, you will <u>rearrange the second deck to the best of your memory</u> to look like the first one, and <u>place the cards face down</u>. You will then ask the audience member that arranged the second deck to come over to you, and you will compare your memorized deck to the second one that you just re-arranged. Each of you will, one at a time, take each card from the top, and lay them out next to each other in two piles, one for your deck and one for theirs. You will see if your first card matches the first card in the other deck and proceed all the way through until you are done. This audience member will be thrilled as they will have witnessed two decks of cards looking identical to each other at the same time right in front of their eyes.

One last memory act that I have just recently started using in regards to cards, is one that sometimes baffles audiences and makes them think that I am cheating (I assure you that I never cheat when it comes to memory). In this trick, you will ask an audience member to shuffle the deck a few times and then lay the cards face down on the table. Make sure the rest of the audience is sitting close enough so that they can all see what you are doing. In this instance, you are going to cover your eyes and not look at the deck. Instead, you will ask the audience volunteer, provided they are honest and trustworthy and have some basic knowledge about playing cards, to pick up each card from the top of the deck, say the name of the card out loud so that everyone can hear it, hold it up high for others to see, and then place that card face up on the table.

You will be listening to the name of each card and trying to recall the information using your ears. If you cannot accurately hear the person or you were unsure of what the volunteer said, ask them to repeat themselves at least once. Once you are done with the deck, you can ask the person to flip the deck face down now, so that the first card you listened to is now on top. Then, with your eyes still closed, call out the name of the first card, have the audience volunteer hold it up so that the others can see, and proceed accordingly throughout the entire deck until finished. I guarantee you that this trick usually shocks audiences as they feel that it is either magic or that you simply have photographic memory (you can decide what to tell them if they ask about either one).

Now, once you are done using the cards, perhaps you could try to challenge your memory with some different field of information. The next topic of memory that I often use in my demonstrations involves memorizing numbers. This will include the need for a chalk board, smart board, large poster or just a big piece of paper, as well as a marker or pen. Also, you will usually need at least 5 or more people for this trick, as just two or three does not seem like much of a challenge. For my first act of numbers memory, I will usually ask each member of the audience to call out a different four-digit number, and then I will write out such information on the paper, from left to right. At this point, I know that I have an even number of numbers to remember, and I already have all of my 100 characters or images fresh in my mind.

As I am looking away from the board, I will ask an audience volunteer to time me to see how long it takes for me to memorize all the numbers. Then, I look at the board and start memorizing all of the numbers going from left to right. Once I am done, I will then ask the audience volunteer to point at the board or the paper as I close my eyes, and then I mentally recall each of the numbers, slowly and one at a time. I will tell that person that I am going only from left to right and I also will occasionally stop to make sure that the person is on track with my recall (don't go too fast in this act). Make sure your audience is paying attention to the volunteer and the board, and not you. This will allow the audience to feel as though they are in a classroom following the teacher's lesson, and they will be most impressed with your ability for sequential number recall.

For my next numbers memory act, I will usually ask a volunteer to come up to the board or the poster with a marker and to write the numbers down for me. Try to have at least 5 or more members of an audience for this one. In the previous trick, you were the one that wrote all of the numbers yourself as you were listening to the audience, this gave you the advantage of already seeing the numbers one at a time as you wrote them, thereby making it easier to recall. In this instance, your volunteer will ask each member of the audience to call out a four-digit number while you are facing away from the poster or the board. This volunteer will be writing down the information as they go. You will still have your eyes open but you will not be looking at the board until everyone has had a turn. Then, once everyone has called out a number, you will then turn around and glance at the board while someone is timing you.

Once you have finished memorizing all of the information, then turn back around again away from the board. After this, you will then recall the actual order of the numbers from front to back and then again from back to front. Make sure that the volunteer knows the order that you are prepared to recall the information in, take a break for a minute after your initial recall of the numbers from front to back, and then announce to the audience that you are going to recall the numbers again backwards. Make sure you keep your eyes away from the board or at least cover your eyes with your hands. Then go ahead and recite the numbers in reverse order with the volunteer following along with each digit. Again, this will definitely impress the audience as they now realize that you are now memorizing information under pressure without any preparation.

Another memory challenge that you can take on with regards to numbers, is the ability to recall numbers <u>without actually seeing them, but only **hearing** them</u>. In this case, you will have a volunteer at the board doing all the writing. You will have <u>each member of the audience call out a different 4-digit number</u>. Since you won't be able to see who is talking at any given time, you must rely that each person only goes once and does not copy off someone else. During this time, your eyes will be closed, and you will be visualizing each set up numbers as you listen to them, one at a time. Ask each person to say their numbers slowly and clearly, so that you can hear each individual digit, repeat more than once if needed. The volunteer should be listening as well so that he or she can correctly write the numbers on the board or paper.

Once everyone is finished, continue to keep your eyes closed and then recite the numbers out loud both forward and backwards. Make sure the volunteer points to each number as your call them out loud and to also put slash marks after each fourth digit. Then, if you are really interested in amazing the group, try to remember the fact that each person gave out a 4-digit number. This means that there should be only 4 numbers at each individual location in your memory palace. This will let you be able to locate and recall any singular group of 4 digits of numbers anytime you want to, such as only reciting the first group of 4 numbers or the second group of the next 4 numbers. Ask anyone to quiz you on the exact order for any of the previous 4 digit groups of numbers, and then recall each group of numbers with perfect accuracy (first four numbers, then last four numbers, etc). Now, your audience will assume that you do in fact have photographic memory at this point, try to revel in this exhilaration.

One last memory stunt that I usually end with when it comes to numbers is my ultimate favorite. In this instance, you will not need a volunteer or a board to write on. All you will need is your audience to sit in a circle or a semi-circle (usually better if you have 5 or more people). In this case, you will ask each person out loud to say a 4- digit number and to remember it for themselves. Since most of us are able to recall at least 7-8 numbers at any given time, this should not be too hard for each person. As each person is reciting their number, make sure you chose people from either left to right or right to left in this case, as some people tend to switch their seats, and this can throw you off. Be sure you are listening carefully to each person, hearing the numbers and linking the pictures for each set of numbers to the order of the individual persons themselves.

For example, for the first person you call upon please try to have their information stored in the first location in one of your memory palaces, and so on. Make sure each person rehearses their individual numbers to themselves so that they too do not forget them. Once everyone is done, point at each individual person, and out loud say the 4-digit number that they each have called. You can either do this in direct order or randomly pick different people from one side to another, as long as they still sitting in the correct order of seats from the beginning. Then, just to have a little more fun, try to repeat some of the 4-digit numbers in reverse for some of the participants, to prove that you have completely remembered all of the information perfectly. This usually gets me some laughs and applauses from the people as they are all impressed that I was listening so intently. (some even try to give me their phone numbers)

Now, lets us try to get away from numbers and cards for a while, and start focusing on a different memory subject, such as vocabulary words. This is the area of memory performance that I usually save for the end of my act, as people are most impressed when I can recall actual literal information as opposed to digits and cards. For this act, you will need something to write with. For my first vocabulary memory stunt, I will usually go up to the board and number it from 1-30. Then, I will look at the audience and ask them to each call out a different English vocabulary word, and then I will write it on the board or poster in front of me. If possible, try to use nouns, verbs and adjectives for this one, so that you are really testing your abilities. You can choose to use either the link method or the memory palace method for this trick, whichever is easier.

Then, once all the words are listed on the board, please have someone time you to see how long it takes for you to memorize the whole list. When you are done memorizing, turn away from the board and ask the audience to direct their attention to the words on the board. Keeping your eyes facing away or covered, proceed to recall all of the words from start to finish, and make sure <u>you actually spell out most of them</u> if they are long just to prove to the audience that you are familiar with the English language. At this point, I usually get some hugs and handshakes from people who are grateful to witness my amazingly accurate literary acumen and my spelling abilities.

For my next vocabulary memory trick, I then ask another volunteer from the audience (again, try to have at least 5 or more people for this one) to come up to the board and number it from 1-30. This time, you will have your eyes directed away from the board. At this point, you will call on each person in the audience to give you another word, upon which the volunteer will write the words on the board behind you. During this time, you will be looking away from the board. Continue doing this until there are 30 different words written on the board. Now, once that is done, immediately turn your head around, <u>have someone start timing you</u>, and then memorize all the words on the board or poster. When you are done memorizing, turn back around again and stop the timer. Then, after you either look away from the board or cover your eyes, proceed to carefully recall all of the words from <u>front to back</u> and then again from <u>back to front</u>, as well as spelling a few words in between. Now, your audience will be really impressed once they realize that you are again remembering vocabulary information while under pressure.

Another memory demonstration that I like to give to people when it comes to English vocabulary is a trick where you ask the audience to sit in either a row or a semi-circle. You will not be using a board or paper for this stunt. During this trick, you will ask each person to say out loud <u>4 different vocabulary words</u>, either nouns or verbs or adjectives. Try to use at least one memory room or location for each group of four words and try to make up a story about them if possible. Do this for each and every person in the audience. Do not write any of this information down, and please ask each person in the audience to repeat their own information quietly to themselves at least once or twice, so that they don't forget their own answers. This will also help the audience with their own individual auditory memory skills.

Once this is done, please point at each person one at a time and then recall the vocabulary words <u>both forwards and backwards for each individual person in the audience</u>. You don't have to do this in any particular order, as you can call on random people in any order you want. This means that you can try to remember the second group of 4 words (or the second person), followed by the last group of 4 words if you want (or the last person), and then change up the order as needed. If you really want to confuse your audience, try to say some of their words in reverse order to see if they truly remember them in the first place. Let them know ahead of time that you will be doing this as you don't want them to think that you were wrong in the first place. This usually leaves the audience in a trance, as they are overwhelmed by the possibility of you being able to recall that many vocabulary words without even looking.

One other memory trick that I like to do for my audience involves using some props, such as a book that I have probably already read earlier in the day or week. Before you do this act, make sure you have already read at least the first 100 pages of your book (either fiction or non-fiction), and that the words are clear and legible to see. For this trick, you only have to read the <u>first sentence of each page of the book</u>, and try to find a certain <u>key word</u>, or a "peg word", that stands out amongst all the other words in the first sentence. It could be a name or a noun, as these are easiest to remember. Try to <u>link the number of the page</u> with an image from one of your 100 original characters or images, and then <u>connect that one peg word to the image</u>. If page 01 has a word in the first sentence such as "cartridge", I will envision an Eagle Scout (**01**) holding a <u>cartridge</u>. Do this for each of your original 100 number characters and then try to make sure that you pick a word from the first sentence of each page that will stick out amongst the rest, and just connect each number character image to each peg word.

This will usually take at least 30-45 minutes before you do this trick, so take your time to read the book and be prepared for it.

Now, once you know that you have already read at least the first sentence of the first 100 pages of the book (get a good-sized book with at least 200 or more pages in it), tell your audience that you have memorized the exact phrases of the first 100 pages of your book, and that you want them to quiz you on it. Ask each member of the audience to pick any page between pages 1-100 in the book, hand the book over to them, and then ask that person to turn to that selected page and only read the first few sentences very slowly and clearly. Close your eyes and listen carefully for the peg word to come up in their first sentence. Make sure the person is reading the sentence loud and slowly.

Once you hear your peg word, allow the person to keep reading for a few more seconds, so as to make such person think that you are still listening to them, when in reality you already should know the exact number of the page. At this point, stop the person from reading and let them know the page number that is associated with the sentences that they are reading. They will be amazed to believe that you have memorized an entire book, when in reality all you did was just memorize a certain word for the first sentence of each page. Try to keep this a secret to yourself for now, unless your audience asks you to remember each word of the book. Then you might have some trouble, but for now, just enjoy the looks on their faces.

Lastly, after you have entertained your group audience members with your skills in the areas of numbers, words, and cards, try to end off your demonstration by performing one final category of memory supremacy, specifically the field of personal data information. This usually works best if you have members in the audience that you don't know too personally. If they are relatives or friends of yours in the group, this trick can be thought of as cheating amongst other strangers in the audience. So, try to pick people that you don't know or are somewhat unfamiliar with. For this trick, ask each person (usually a group or 5 or more people) at least 5 pieces of personal information about themselves that they are okay with sharing. Don't try to ask them for things such as their Social Security or phone numbers, as most strangers are usually nervous about giving out such information.

Instead, ask them simple questions such as nationalities, birthdays, states of residency, or job and educational degrees.

Try to write this information on a board or paper in either columns or rows, with each one labeled with the name of the person on top. Then after all information is written down, have someone time you as you look at the board. Use one memory palace for each person, with a different piece of information for each different location in your palace, and also use the same order of personal data for each person so that you always know what categories you are looking for. Once you have completely memorized all of the information, turn around and look at each person, and then call out all of their personal information in exact order. Make sure you ask whether or not you are right after each answer, to which each person will probably nod their heads and start smiling as you get more and more information correct. Try to compliment such people on certain things that you find outstanding or admirable about them, as this will win you more smiles and cheers, as well as a few new friends if possible.

Another trick that you can use with regards to personal data can be done with the help of a volunteer, who will not be giving out any personal information of their own for this act. In this instance, you will be asking another group of at least 5 or more people to give out different types of personal information about themselves, such as jobs, favorite foods, hobbies, children or marital status, and zip codes of their addresses. For this performance, the volunteer will be writing this information on the board while you are facing away from it, making sure to label each column for each person, and writing down the information in a list format. Once you have at least 5 pieces of information for at least five strangers, turn around and look at the board while someone times you to see how long it would take to remember all the information for all the people. As soon as you are done, have the person or volunteer stop timing you. Then look at the chosen audience members one at a time, and then recall all of the personal information out loud to each of the listed spectators. This again will definitely delight and astonish the entire group to think that you can remember so much personal information about a group of strangers in such a short amount of time.

And finally, the very last trick that I like to use to give people the idea that I have the greatest memory in the world is when I combine my personal information memory techniques with my name and faces memory skills. At the beginning of this demonstration, you will write down the <u>12 different categories</u> of personal information, or <u>the Lovings Dozens</u>, on the board or poster, in a list format. After this, you will not be writing down any more information on the board or the poster. You will have to use your listening and concentration skills for this act. You will not need a timer for this act as you will be doing a lot of talking to people and cannot be sure how fast the information will be presented to you. To prepare for this act, I usually chose at least <u>10 members of the audience</u> that I do not know or are unfamiliar with (the more the better), and then I chose to remember at least 4 random pieces of personal information about each person.

To make your audience feel more relaxed, <u>let each person decide what category of information they wish</u> to share with you, as long as it pertains to the 12 categories of information that you have already listed. Some people might even trust you to know their phone numbers or addresses, if they feel calm enough around you. Tell them to give you at least <u>4 different pieces of personal data</u> about each one of them, and make sure you ask the person for their first names. Put the first persons' information in your first memory palace, second person's information in a second memory palace, and so on. Once you are done interviewing all of the 10 people (between 5-10 is a good number, as you will have between 30-40 bits of personal data), take a few moments and close your eyes and relax. Let the audience think that you are unable to completely recall the information, as this usually leaves them in suspense.

At this point, look at any person in the audience, point to that person, and then recall out loud all the pieces of personal information that were shared for that one person, in the exact order that they were given to you. Then do the same thing for each and every chosen member of your audience. This lets the audience know that you were listening along with all their stories. Don't be surprised if you get lots of hugs, handshakes and even a few kisses from people, as they will now believe that not only do you have the greatest memory in the world, but that you are now their new best friend due to your personal knowledge of them.

CHAPTER 17

Climbing the mountain of memory, now what?

Previously, when I was attending my first ever national memory competition back in 2018, there were many former winners and contestants there, most of whom I already had heard about through my intensive interest about memory sports. I had looked up names of past winners and finalists and was amazed to see a few of my favorite "celebrity" competitors in the same room as me. One of those memory athletes, whom I had heard a lot of great news about, was a young, strong and tall adult male previous winner with the initials of N.D.

What struck me as the most memorable about this particular individual was not just how many different names and faces memory records he had previously set, or the fact that he had won this specific tournament at least 4 times in the past (the current record for most wins at USA memory is still 4, one more win and he breaks the record), but the fact that in his spare time, he enjoys climbing the highest mountains all over the world. And this made me think of one very important question that many of us ask ourselves when we have finally achieved our dreams in life, or in his case, when we finally <u>make it to the top of the mountain</u>. And that question is, what do I do now after I have accomplished my goals?

In the field of psychology and social work, there is a concept known as **self-actualization**. This is an internal state of mind, where the person feels as though they have achieved, accumulated, and accomplished everything that they have ever set before themselves to do. Normally, the first thing that we want to acquire is materials for our physical well-being, then we look towards receiving emotional support and nurturance from others, as well as also developing a positive sense of self-esteem through our life experiences. (if you are wondering where this comes from, look up Maslow's Hierarchy of Needs). However, very few of us will ever achieve the highest level of self-fulfillment or accomplishment in life known as self-actualization. What this means is that if we set a goal for ourselves to achieve, and we later achieve or accomplish it, what do we do afterwards? Do we just sit around and do nothing? Or do we try to challenge ourselves further to see how much "higher" or further we can go? This might make more sense in the field of either work or physical health, as we are always looking to either further ourselves or thrive harder to achieve things as we get older. However, when it comes to mountain climbing, once you get to the top of the mountain, and there are no more peaks or summits yet to climb, the biggest question to ask yourself is this: Now what do I do?

That is a question that I asked myself after I had learned all of the basic tools and techniques of memory improvement and was able to effectively demonstrate such skills and techniques not only to myself but to others. Still, I always wondered, after I had learned everything that could be learned on this particular subject of cognitive enhancement, what was I going to do next to challenge myself? And then I realized, like most therapists in this world regularly do every day in their practices, that I needed to develop or create some type of "treatment" goals or plans for myself, so that I could have something to not only strive for, but also to help keep me motivated and working towards improving myself.

And with that in mind, I started to create several goals or "treatment" plans for myself (yes, I do this all the time for my clients), that were measurable, objective, and achievable within a certain period of time. While most of us in life have our own life goals that we want to strive for due to our own reasons, let me share with you some of the things that you can achieve simply by just using the memory skills that I have taught you, and decide for yourself if you would really like to see how far up the "mountain" you can really climb.

As far as I know, there are three main areas in life that you can improve upon by using your new memory skills that you could never have achieved before just by using your old memory skills. Those three areas in your life are classified as **work, family and education**. Either you can use these mnemonic techniques to succeed at work with clients and colleagues, at home with family and friends, or at school with tests and quizzes. We are all different people at different stages in our lives, with multiple expectations placed on us almost every day. The possibilities of what we can do or work on are endless. And most of us would be ever so grateful if we could find a way to improve our ability to handle the demands of our lives with much greater ease. So, for now, let's try to focus on what goals you can set for yourselves in each of these three different areas of life, and see for yourself where you would like to get started.

First, when it comes to **education**, there were three previous chapters where I talked to you about how to memorize poetry and speeches, vocabulary words, as well as materials from books. Though these chapters do not explain everything about every problem or subject that will come your way, these chapters do provide some ideas and guidance that can be used in order to help future students spend less time studying and get better grades with less stress. Plus using the Charting Method of Note Taking can also be used for the same purposes. Try to imagine how great it would be to be able to spend half as much time studying and get twice as many A's on your tests and quizzes. By utilizing the lessons from these three chapters and by using the memory palace or link methods described before, just realize how easy it would be to memorize all the necessary information for a future test or quiz. You could be able to spend time in the days before an exam in your home, going over your notes and using these memory techniques, instead of tirelessly reading over the same information again and again, hoping that it will stick (rote memorization). You can now actually have some fun and joy during studying for tests and quizzes, while at the same time getting rewarded with better grades in school.

I guarantee you that the information will stick in your head longer and easier as long as you use the methods already described, as well the lesson on long-term memory, and the charting method of notes. Also, try to reserve <u>only one memory palace for each of the core subjects</u> that you are studying. Make sure that you keep using the same palace each time a new test or quiz comes up, as you will usually have at least two to three weeks between examinations for the same subject. That way, when the next test or quiz for a particular class comes up, by the time this comes up, the information from the previous lesson will probably have faded away. And you can feel free to use that same memory palace again in order to fill in the new information (remember the chalk board scenario from earlier with regards to reusing memory palaces too quickly).

So, one major goal that many of us you who are still in high school or college could try to work on while using the memory palace techniques, is to see if you can try to either "raise your GPA at least one letter grade" or perhaps "finish your studies" early enough so that you have time during the day to work on other things. Imagine the possibility of being on the honor roll or the dean's list each semester, or having other colleges or universities offering you the best scholarships and financial incentives out there due to your high grades. Either way, you are winning or gaining something by using the memory techniques to help you in your academic or educational endeavors.

Now for those of you who have finished school, and are now actively **working at your job**, you are a lot like me. I am just another member of the adult workforce, struggling each day to keep up with the demands and expectations of working an 8 hour shift, constantly bombarded with endless responsibilities and assignments and hoping not to lose my mind before I go home at the end of the day. Well, I can tell that by using the memory lessons that were provided to you in the chapters earlier regarding personal data, names and faces, and numbers, you can probably accomplish more work in less time and be able to handle any additional responsibilities that come your way, just by focusing on these three domains. For example, if you spend lots of time dealing with other people at your job, such as colleagues, clients, customers, patients, or consumers, think about how much better you will perform at your job duties simply by being able to remember numbers, personal data, and names and faces.

Let's say for example that you work in a field where your salary or job performance depends upon the quality of your interactions with other clients or customers who want to be serviced by you. Think about if you could remember their names, personal information, and any related numbers that are applicable to their case. Just imagine the looks on their faces when they realize that you took the time to get to know more about them, instead of just treating them like another nameless droid. You will see a great change in that particular person, as well as with your other colleagues and supervisors, as all parties will not only be impressed with your work performance, but also will feel as though you can handle more responsibilities at the job. You could possibly receive either a raise or a promotion, depending on where you work. So, instead of climbing the "mountain" of memory sports, you would be climbing the corporate "ladder" of success at your own job site. And each time you succeed at doing something and get promoted for it, try to see how much further you can go in your current vocational adventure.

For example, perhaps you are someone who works in a field where you have to remember lots of specific information about a particular client or a company. You could remember things such as financial amounts, account numbers, statistics, percentages or office numbers. Simply using number memory along with name and face memory is all that you need for such. If you already know that a particular client is coming in to see you in a business or financial institution, and you want to remember how much money they have, as well as their account numbers, changes in interest rates, or the phone numbers of other employees that can assist you, simply just use the number memory system and try to link all the information to the name and face of the person.

Start by using their name and face in the first memory palace room, then create images for other numerically related items, especially if you have the information already in front of you in the form of either a chart or a table. (use the charting method of note taking for this particular challenge). When your client comes to see you, and you already know all of their financial information before the person even gets a chance to ask you how your day was, they will be so amazed by your diligence and abilities that they will feel as if you are the only person they can trust with their numbers. Also, if you have to use the same principle to recall financial statistics about a particular <u>business or company</u>, either internal or external, simply use the same methods from before and watch your boss and colleagues be impressed with your ability to know so much about your business as well as others.

Also, if you are someone who is working in a business where you have to be able to make presentations or remember important information about a particular product or commodity, you can still use the memory palace system to be better prepared for such anxiety ridden job expectations. Many people report feeling scared or nervous when they have to get up in front of a group of people and try to convince such audience about their competence in any major field or subject they are talking about. By using the techniques from the speeches memory section, you can recall all of your notes about your presentation before you actually get up and start talking. Plus, by using names and faces memory techniques, you can also make your audience like you more by remembering who they are instead of just calling them "sir" or "miss". Think about how confident and self-assured you will feel once you have easily convinced a group of people about your particular idea or product, by remembering everything you can about your particular product, as well as some related personal stuff about the people you are talking to. In no time at all, you will be the most popular and sought-after expert in your company and will be making friends with some very important and high-ranking people, who can take your career to new "heights".

Sometimes, the objective of your job is your ability to sell something to one of your customers, such as a product, a service, or some other type of business related correspondence. And that for each successful deal or negotiation that is made between you and this potential future client, you could possibly be rewarded with either a commission check, a raise in pay, or perhaps even a promotion. In this case, the best method to use for such business related purposes are the personal data memory section, as well as the smaller section on customer service complaints. In this instance, you could either be told ahead of time that a particular client is coming in to see you about the possibility of buying your product, or you might just happen to bump into such person in the aisles of your store.

Either way, try to take the time to get to know some personal information about each customer, and also try to remember what their purposes or concerns are in regards to your particular products or services. Then, using some business skills and social fluency, try to recite back all of the information that they told you about themselves, including their names if this was already mentioned. I guarantee you, this particular customer will want to work with you and nobody else, and would be willing to listen to you more attentively in regards to your potential sales pitch. This gives you the opportunity to convince the other person that you are somebody worth trusting of their monies, and they will more than likely be willing to either purchase something from you, or perhaps negotiate some type of transaction. Either way, you will now have a new client and a possible financial reward coming from your supervisors at a later date.

Or perhaps you are just one of those people who are <u>struggling to keep up with</u> the endless piles of work that are literally accumulating on your desk each day. And you silently wish that there was some magic to make sense of such an overwhelming and unending source of stress. Well now, there is a way to pull yourself out of the rubble of paperwork that is drowning you each day and finally be able to lift your head "above water". If you try to use the memory system that was described earlier regarding how to <u>remember important dates and appointments, as well as remembering assignments</u>, you will find that things become much easier for you at the job. Although this will not stop the workflow from coming through your desk, it will definitely make the work itself so much easier for you.

Instead of simply jotting down hundreds of important entries into your date book and feeling as though there are not enough hours in a day to complete the tasks at hand, you will see that, by using your previously described mnemonic techniques, your brain will be able to have its own internal "date book". This will allow you to be consciously aware of what needs to be done at any given time, and you will be more prepared and ready to work on such items later, rather than simply going through an inordinately long check off list of things yet to work on. This will make you feel as though you have more power and control over your work life now than you ever thought before.

No longer will you ever feel as though it is impossible to remember a specific deadline or a vitally important meeting, or perhaps work on a problem that needs to be solved soon. Now, you will have the limitless ability to be able to multi-task in your head, taking care of any requests that come your way, without feeling like your brain is about to explode. You will start to see acknowledgments and appreciation from your supervisors and colleagues, as they will see that you are better able to handle your job with less stress and are more productive in completing and handing in your work on time. (Now suddenly, the idea of staying afloat seems to make more sense, huh?)

And just because you are either working or going to school, does not mean that you can't have a **personal life** of your own once the final bell rings, or the clock strikes 5pm. Perhaps you want to improve relationships with friends or family when you are done with your day, or perhaps you are retired and enjoying the peacefulness of waking of late and going to bed whenever you want. Either way, you might still feel as though you want to improve certain aspects of your personal life as well, only to discover that your memory does not allow you to accomplish such individual tasks so easily. Well, don't be too worried about it. You already have learned some lessons previously that will help you in such endeavors. In the chapter regarding personal usage of memory techniques, you were taught about how to remember things like appointments, chores, and other domestic related concerns.

By using these lessons and the memory palace method, you will have less stress in your personal life as you will be able to remember important things that seem to annoy you most when you accidentally forget them. If you want to be able to recall when your loved one has to go to an appointment, or how much time you have to pay your bills and do your chores, then all you have to do is use the systems described previously, and see how much smoother and easier such irritable daily responsibilities become. You will not feel as tired and angry and upset as you normally would if you forget something very important. You will probably feel as though you can handle more stress easier than you ever did before. This will greatly improve your relationships with your family and friends, as you will not dread seeing them again or trying to help them solve another domestic related problem. Instead you will feel confident enough to step up and handle whatever challenge comes your way.

In addition to personal family life, one of the most wonderful things that you can do for your family throughout the course of your lifetime is to <u>try to remember important personal data</u> about your friends and loved ones. If you want to recall about each member of <u>your family's personal information</u>, you already know how to use the <u>Loving Dozen lessons</u>. Instead of writing such information in an address book or a sheet of paper, either of which can be lost or discarded, simply use the memory palace technique for each person in your immediate life, and that is all you need. You can also try to use their own home or apartment, only if you have actually seen it before, as a tool for a memory palace. You can store several pieces of related personal data about each person in each palace; such as family relations, favorite foods, jobs, or other related accomplishments. Think of it as each person's individual "<u>family storage cabinet</u>".

Just imagine how wonderful your relatives would feel if you were able to recall their birthdays as well as their own personal achievements, anytime you ever saw them when they come over for a visit. They would feel so welcome and special in your presence, and this would greatly improve the status of your relationships. Plus, if ever anybody in your family ever moved or relocated, even if you don't get a chance to see their new place, simply just ask them what their new address or phone number is and store that new information in their individual "family storage cabinet" and update it as needed. That way, you are always remaining alert and up to date on what is going on in the lives of those you love and cherish the most, instead of being one of those relatives who keeps asking questions about things that happened years and years ago.

Or maybe you are just one of those people who are not interested in using memory techniques for personal, vocational or academic affairs. Maybe you are just interested in possibly competing in various memory tournaments, putting on memory related performance and demonstrations, or perhaps you just would like to be a better poker player. No matter what you want to do or why you want to do it, <u>the</u> <u>choice is completely up to you</u>. I personally still use a few of the mnemonic techniques, both for home and at work (I am not in school and will probably not be going back anytime soon). Plus, I also continue to practice my memory techniques constantly so that I can better prepare for any future memory tournaments or championships, whether they are in person or on the computer (I do online competitions a lot these days to stay in my competitive mode). Regardless of whatever reason you have for using these cognitive enhancement techniques and skills, there is one result that is always the same: **YOU WILL ALWAYS IMPROVE AS TIME GOES ON AND AS YOU CONTINUE TO PRACTICE**. This is the one area of life where getting older does not mean getting slower. The longer you keep using these skills, the faster and better you then become at memory challenges. You will continue to amaze yourself each time you set another milestone for yourself and later overcome it. You will soon realize, just like in the movie "Limitless", that there is really nothing you cannot do once you set your mind to achieving it.

I remember a line from the short-lived TV series "Limitless", which was also based upon the movie. In that particular TV series, the main character is a man named Brian Finch. Brian Finch is a young man who is struggling with making money for his family and trying to start a career for himself. One day, he meets with an old college friend named Eli, who gives him a sample of the infamous memory drug from the original movie called "NZT 48". At the time, he is working a temp job at a local business for just a few weeks, where his job is to basically read through hundreds of employee files and try to determine which employees are responsible for causing potentially criminal issues of sexual harassment at the job site. At first, he believes that this job will perhaps take him two weeks to complete, and that he will probably either quit the job due to the frustration of such work, or possibly lose his mind due to reading such a large amount of boring and mundane corporate paperwork.

However, as soon as he takes the NZT drug, he begins to feel the "limitless" effect in his head. He is then able to sort through all of the information in the employee files in just about two hours. He is able to demonstrate perfect recall of all of the employees' personal information without even trying, as well as being able to create a new filing system to be used for all future personnel issues by using a color coding system. In addition, he also gives some much-needed career guidance to the attractive female staffer who is assigned to work with him, as well as being able to flirt with her a little. As soon as he steps out of the office and into the streets of New York, he utters a line to himself as he is walking away, that clearly defines what this particular chapter is really all about. He says, "*I remember thinking, the world is mine, I just have to decide what I want to do with it*".

And that is **the feeling that I want you** to have once you have read through all of these chapters and have learned all of the techniques that you feel you need (minus taking any non-FDA experimental nootropic pills; trust me- the withdrawal effects of NZT were horrendous) What I would like for you to experience, once you are comfortable with your own current regimen of memory training, is the feeling that Brian had once he left the office that day and walked down to Columbus Square, where he later entertained the crowds with his new profound ability to play a guitar, and his genius level strategies in playing stress chess. And that feeling is "**THE WORLD IS YOURS, YOU JUST HAVE TO DECIDE WHAT YOU WANT TO DO WITH IT**". And what better weapon to use, for such an enormous and daunting challenge such as this, than with the most highly advanced weapon in the whole world: **your brain**.

FINAL TEST

Well, I bet right about now you are either feeling very comfortable and confident in terms of your mental abilities, or maybe I have just simply figured out a way to completely burn you out due to the sheer amount of coursework included in these pages. Either way, before you go ahead and give yourself a break from all of these mental Olympics, <u>I have one final memory challenge for you</u>. The reason I offer this challenge to you is to see if you have what it takes to make it to the USA National Memory Championship. The types of challenges that you are about to be offered are the types of challenges that most nationally and internationally ranked mnemonists and memory athletes have been able to achieve to win their memory titles. I will be using the **same original topics of memory** that were introduced to you during your **initial challenge** at the beginning of the book. And just to see how far you have gotten with regards to your newly discovered memory talents, <u>I have changed some of the rules and regulations</u> of your upcoming memory tests, just to see if you really have want it takes to be a national memory competitor. So, get out a few more pieces of paper, pens, and a stop watch, because it's time for **the final round** of your memory course work.

First, as you remember from your initial challenge at the beginning of this book, I led off with a memory challenge involving **how to memorize numbers**. Previously I listed the numbers as either singular, double or pairs of numbers spaced next to each other. This time, I am giving you exactly <u>5 lines with exactly 20 numbers for each line</u>, for a grand total of **100 numbers to memorize**. And this time, the numbers are spaced closely to each other. But don't worry; I made sure that the same amount was listed for each line. You will need two sheets of paper, a pencil, and a timer. In this exercise, you will need to copy the numbers on one sheet of paper, but make sure you **do NOT put any spaces or slash marks** between any of the numbers, as this would make it too easy for you to recall. Then, once you have all the numbers written out on one sheet of paper, turn this page over for a few seconds. Then take out your stop watch, flip the page over again, and start timing yourself. See if you can use either your finger or your pen to make sure you follow along correctly with the list of digits. For this exercise, **you will have only 5 minutes** for the memorization part. This will obviously be done after you have already copied the original digits down and started the timer.

After the 5 minutes is over, flip over such paper again, and use your other sheet to record your answers. You will have <u>10 minutes for this recall</u>, so that you have enough time to write out your answers and make any corrections (use a pencil if needed). Remember, there are only 20 numbers per line, so if you use lined paper for this exercise, make sure you count to see if you have written the exact number of digits necessary for each line of your answers. And for the scoring for this exercise, you will get a maximum of <u>20 points for each line </u>that you get perfectly correct. If you make <u>one mistake on any line, you get 0 points</u>, which means that the line does not count.

This is the same method that is used at the national and world championships, so the pressure is on. You can also leave a blank space if you don't remember a certain number on a line as you will only get credit for how many total numbers per line you actually get correct. And you will only get <u>one shot at this</u>; do not try to do this exercise multiple times in the same day. If you wish to repeat it again, simply put it away and try it another day under the same conditions. So for now, give yourself a minute to relax and decide for yourself when you would like to start this first exercise. If you need to go over your number character images and needed memory palaces before you attempt this, go right ahead. If not, then get ready, get set, and go for it.

76945813584265588474 = total

71234569889699954146 = total

20025580254013549841 = total

20684475769876254101 = total

03594861200546452824 = total

Next, we are going to test your memory for **memorizing playing cards**. Now, for this exercise, what I am going to need for you to do is to go and find a deck of cards and shuffle it a few times (at least 3-4 times using a ruffle shuffle). This will take some time, but don't worry; you are creating your own base deck. Now, once the cards are shuffled accordingly, take out another piece of paper and write down the list of the following cards that I have presented to you below. You can list them from 1-52 in either one row or two, whichever way you would prefer. Then, once you have listed all the cards in the correct order, flip the paper over so that you cannot see it, and <u>then re-shuffle the deck again</u> so that the cards are completely out of order from the original ending. (<u>do this 1-2 times using a ruffle shuffle</u>).

This will probably throw you off, but that is the part of the memory test. At this point, your cards will be out of order and you will have no frame of reference from what they looked like before. After you have shuffled the deck, take out your stop watch and flip over the paper with the cards you previously listed. Give yourself **5 minutes to look through the list of card names that you wrote**. If you finish early, stop the timer and right down the time you finished. Once this is done, flip the paper over so that you cannot see your answers. Then take out the deck that you now have shuffled multiple times, and look through the cards. Try to **manually rearrange the cards** from this deck to match the list of cards that you have already just memorized. You will have about <u>5 minutes for this recall</u>, so make sure your timer is nearby. This is done in the national and international championships all the time, as mental athletes will have to memorize one deck of cards, then place that deck face down, and then rearrange another base deck to match the original.

Once you are done with your recall, flip back over the answer paper with the cards listed so that you can see them. Compare your rearranged deck of cards to the list below. If you get one card wrong, only count that score up until that card, so if you got the 28th card wrong, your score would therefore be a 28. And again, don't try this task more than once in the same day, as you will probably remember it better the more times you try it. Simply put it away and try it again the following day so that most of the information is forgotten out of your head. Take a minute and go over your card memory lessons as well as any memory palaces that you are prepared to use. If you are okay for now, then get ready, get set, and go for it.

1	3 of Diamonds			26	Queen of Spades
2	10 of Spades			27	3 of Spades
3	4 of Clubs			28	Ace of Clubs
4	9 of Spades			29	Queen of Diamonds
5	2 of Clubs			30	9 of Hearts
6	Jack of Clubs			31	5 of Diamonds
7	5 of Spades			32	King of Clubs
8	10 of Clubs			33	King of Hearts
9	4 of Spades			34	6 of Diamonds
10	2 of Diamonds			35	Ace of Hearts
11	Queen of Hearts			36	7 of Clubs
12	King of Spades			37	Jack of Diamonds
13	7 of Spades			38	6 of Spades
14	Jack of Spades			39	2 of Hearts
15	King of Diamonds			40	9 of Clubs
16	5 of Clubs			41	Ace of Diamonds
17	2 of Spades			42	8 of Clubs
18	4 of Hearts			43	3 of Hearts
19	7 of Diamonds			44	4 of Diamonds
20	9 of Diamonds			45	8 of Diamonds
21	8 of Hearts			46	Jack of Hearts

22	3 of Clubs			47	5 of Hearts
23	8 of Spades			48	Ace of Spades
24	6 of Clubs			49	Queen of Clubs
25	10 of Diamonds			50	10 of Hearts
				51	6 of Hearts
				52	7 of Hearts

Total=

Finally, for your last major memory test, I am going to quiz you again on the final topic that we chose to do during our initial memory test: **vocabulary word memory**. For this memory test, take out another sheet of paper, and number it from 1-50. For this exercise, you will **NOT be writing down the words** first before you memorize, as this makes it easier for you to recall it as you are doing it. Instead, you **will just number your sheet of paper** and leave it as it is. Then, once you are done, take out a stop watch and start to look through the list of words actually described below in the book itself. You will only have 5 minutes to do this. Once the timer is done, shut the book and start writing your answers down on the answer paper.

You will have about 10 minutes for recall. Make sure you time yourself for the recall period, as some people tend to forget how much time this will take due to spelling and grammar. When the recall time is over, simply open up the book and look through the list that you created in order to check out your answers. Remember that the spelling and grammar is important, so if the word is not completely spelled correct, you get no credit for it. Give yourself 2 points for each correct answer, for a grand total of **100 points maximum**. And again, don't do this exercise more than once a day, simply put it away and try it again the following day once the information is out of your head. Give yourself a minute to pick out a good memory palace for this particular exercise. Get ready, get set, and go for it.

1. archery	25. rescue	49. wedding
2. florist	26. waterfalls	50. permanent
3. abbreviation	27. paper	
4. gnome	28. Vaseline	
5. jousting	29. lashing	
6. formidable	30. vanity	
7. wow	31. orphanage	
8. patience	32. trivial	
9. hell	33. seem	
10. particular	34. questioning	
11. yaks	35. flossing	
12. powdery	36. titrate	
13. sea lions	37. seagull	
14. title	38. merry go round	
15. Indian	39. carnivore	
16. olive	40. rubric's cube	
17. tertiary	41. kite	
18. falafel	42. chemistry	
19. libidinous	43. battalion	
20. xylophones	44. paleontology	
21. petty	45. superfluous	
22. funeral	46. was	
23. union	47. interior	
24. beginners	48. capsize	

TOTAL=

Conclusion

Well, like any good social worker, I always tell my clients that the hardest thing about therapy itself is to terminate services at some point. Eventually all things, whether good or bad, must soon come to an end. And like most of my clients, there comes a time when I tell you that person that there is nothing else for us to work on, and that I must set them free back into the real world, so that they can use our lessons to help them better adjust to life outside of the office. So, with that being said, I think it is time for me to let you go and say good bye at this point. I believe that I have taught you as much as I could through this book and that if you have come this far in your "journey", perhaps you are ready and willing to carry on a little bit further without me. I feel that you are ready to tackle the world of memory alone for now, with a new and fulfilled sense of esteem and pride. As you have learned some very important and life changing skills and techniques in memory, you are now better prepared to handle whatever challenges you thought you were impossible before. But before you leave, let us try to summarize some of the major lessons that I hope you have come to understand from this book. This will help me in order to make sure that you have completely realized what it is I had hoped you would comprehend.

First, I am sure that you already know that, like yourself, I was once a novice memory athlete, who had never heard of the memory palace or link association techniques before. And when I first tried to use such techniques, it was then that I realized that I had stumbled upon something that would forever change my life as well as my own way of thinking. In just a few short years, my brain is capable of doing things I never thought possible even 20 years ago. If someone would have told me that one day, I would be able to complete the final memory tests that were just given to you; I would say that this would seem absolutely impossible. Now, I realize that this special gift is not just reserved for the elite few, but for anyone that makes the effort to actually use these techniques in their own way. Like I said before, **I am just like anybody else in the world, anybody can do this**. And by that realization, I hope that you still feel compelled and motivated to continue to work on your techniques so that one day, hopefully in a few months or so, you too could be sitting right next to me at another national memory championship, against the best in this country. (anybody can sign up around spring of each year for such event)

Second, if you have ever seen a movie about a superhero or some other related DC Comic or Marvel related character, you probably know the meaning of the term "superpowers". Well, superpowers don't just have to be something that only fictional TV, movie, or comic book heroes get to enjoy. You too can now have your own individual superpower of the brain, which is the ability to have a record-setting memory. This is a power where almost no piece of information cannot be stored and retrieved from inside of your head whenever you want to retrieve it. You too can enjoy the feeling of having your own special ability, while those around you can only look on in amazement. Although anybody else can utilize these techniques, you will be many steps ahead of your friends and colleagues, as they will be left in awe of your new amazing talents.

Third, it is hard to believe that this technique has only been around for just a few thousand years, or at least when we first documented the case of Simonides of Ceos. If you think about it, before we had modern things like pencils, paper, books, computers or even a verbal language, we still had to rely upon our memory to help us to survive in such a complex world of information. From creating the first fire, to hunting and gathering, to modern day technological achievements, memory has allowed man to move forward in our evolutionary quest for supreme dominance in this world. Biologically, our brains have not changed in size, structure, or chemical composition in over thousands of years. This tiny, little, 3 pound mass of fatty tissue in your head has remained unchanged for so many generations. However, our brains have also been left partially unused for centuries, as we have always had the abilities to do such mnemonic techniques in our minds, but yet we have never truly known how to access such hidden talents until recently. Well, now the time has come to finally unlock your ancestral innate abilities, and to use such talents, once and for all, in this highly advanced and information soaked world we currently live in.

Fourth, what has always surprised me the most about the usage of memory enhancement techniques, is the realization that none of these mnemonic processes or skills are regularly taught in any major school or institution of learning in this county, such as a high school, technical school, or college university. Occasionally, one select school may possibly teach a short course of such a mnemonic subject for perhaps one semester to a small group of children or teenagers. But that is usually the extent of such educational lessons. Usually, these memory techniques areas are occasionally or briefly mentioned during the course of some school or college related workshop, but no one ever really seems to truly give this field of study the attention or respect that it deserves. Simply just talking about memory techniques or mentioning them in discussion will not help the learner to really be able to grasp the inner workings and dynamics of this field of study.

Most people have to go out to a library, go on the computer, or meet a friend who is interested in the subject, just to get some information on how memory improvement really works. This is unfortunate however as I truly believe that if this type of cognitive instruction could be available to more people either in schools or at work, the world itself would be a much different place than we live in now, as more people from all over the world would be able to demonstrate such advanced mental and cognitive abilities that were once considered rare in this world. Perhaps this book will shed a just a little more light out there to those people who are still using such older methods of memory and learning, and are still continuously struggling to reach some level of intellectual potential.

Fifth, when I finally discovered that I had this unknown and unrealized ability of my mind, I kept wondering how I could have ever lived so long in my life without ever having used this method before. And that is something that I believe that most of you out there are probably thinking about yourselves, once you finally start to see the results of this process working out for you in your own individual lives. Whether it is getting better grades in school, making more money at work, having less stress in your family relations, getting along better with friends and colleagues, or just simply competing in various memory championships; you will soon start to discover just how much better your life truly is now than it ever was before. Realize this, if you stop using these techniques all together for the rest of your life, you will eventually go back to your old ways of thinking and memory. And guaranteed, you will probably produce similar mediocre results when you have to memorize things. The point is this; now that you have this new profound power of the mind, please continue to work hard on using it each day so that you never ever lose such natural abilities when you get older.

Finally, before you start to think that I have given you the key to the "Holy Grail" of your mind, just remember that memory alone is only something, but it is not everything. You must also realize that memory alone just gives you the ability to mechanically spew out a bunch of random pieces of information at will. It does not guarantee that you will completely realize what you are saying or the importance of such information. In order to remedy this issue, you must also strive for both creativity and understanding of everything that you memorize. What I mean by is that not only should you try to memorize information as it is listed, but also try to understand what the actual subject matter truly means to the world, and how you can apply this information in your own personal base.

Sherlock Holmes had different amounts of knowledge about random subjects in his head at any time, but somehow he always figured out a way to utilize such information for his own personal pursuits. He also made sure that he understood why the facts were so important and relevant to him, and then came up with some creative method to incorporate such data into the real world. So, before you assume that you have absolutely nothing left to learn in life, try to do what Sherlock Holmes did and incorporate both understanding and creativity of information into your memorization pursuits. That way, you will be able to explain to others, in your own way, that your way of thinking is truly "elementary".

Well, with all that being said, I think that it is time to finally say goodbye and wish you the best of luck in your future endeavors. It has been an honor and privilege to have worked with you all of these days and weeks. I certainly hope that you have learned some valuable lessons in memory improvement throughout the chapters of this book. I realize that certain subjects are probably harder than others, and that there are some topics that you will probably never have to use in your life. However, this book is organized to serve as a reference guide for people like you who would like to improve their memory in more than once just simple subject. The choice of what exactly you decide to do with all of the different types of knowledge presented in this book is entirely your choice. I am simply giving you the tools for you to use in your own individual pursuits in life.

I truly want to thank you for allowing me to be a part of your "journey" into memory, and to be able to coach you through all of the various lessons that I myself have learned over the years. If you ever feel that you have any questions or concerns about any of the related techniques mentioned previously, or if you just simply need to "refresh" your memory on some random topic of information that you have not familiar with, please go ahead and reread any chapter as often as you would like. I guarantee you that the more times you read and review each lesson, as well as practice each of the skills that were previously listed, the better your memory will become each time. And so with that, I wish you all the best in life, good luck to you all, take care and God bless.

INDEX OF TOPICS

About the Author

Daniel Guilfoyle is a 3 time USA Memory Championship competitor who is capable of memorizing an entire deck of card in just over a minute, as well as recalling over 100 random numbers in only just five minutes. He is a licensed clinic social worker (LCSW) in New York. He works and lives in the city of Middletown. He is married to his wife Erin, they both have three cats; Hedwig, Peaches and Willow. In 2016, after only learning these valuable memory skills for just a few months, Daniel was capable of remembering vast amounts of information with superior recall in just a short amount of time. Learn how this particular individual came to discover the secret to achieving the highest level of memory mastery anybody can possibly realize.